OSPREY COMBAT AIRCRAFT

LOCKHEED SR-71 OPERATIONS IN THE FAR EAST

SERIES EDITOR: TONY HOLMES

OSPREY COMBAT AIRCRAFT • 76

LOCKHEED SR-71 OPERATIONS IN THE FAR EAST

PAUL F CRICKMORE

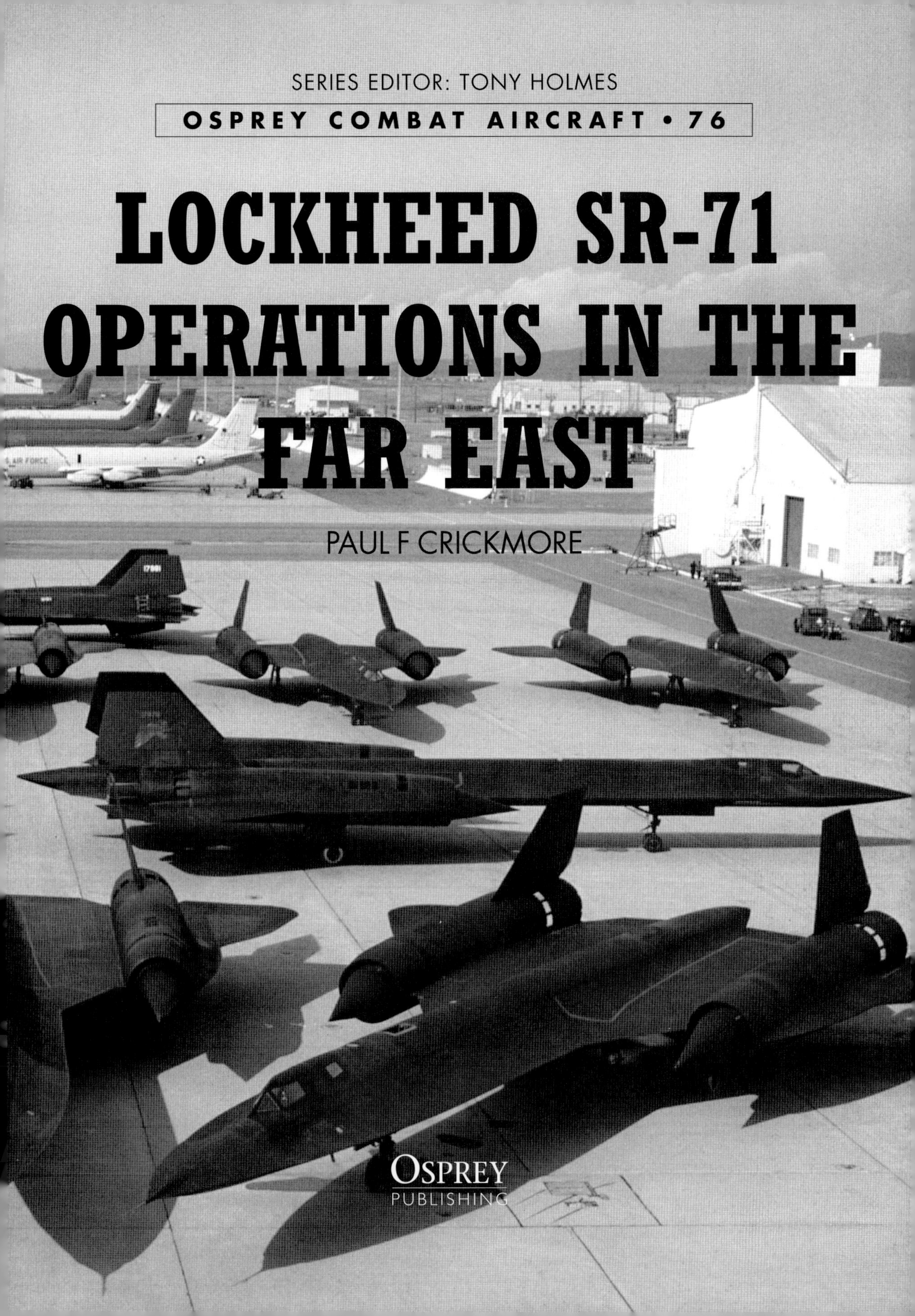

OSPREY
PUBLISHING

Front Cover
SR-71A 64-17976 (Article 2027), call sign 'Beaver Five-Zero', heads 'feet-wet' near the Demilitarised Zone (DMZ) between North and South Vietnam during the SR-71's first operational combat mission on Thursday, 21 March 1968. Having deployed '976' to Kadena air base, on the Japanese island of Okinawa, 11 days earlier, Majs Jerry O'Malley and Ed Payne duly flew the same aircraft on the *Senior Crown* programme's operational debut. They coasted in on a heading of 284 degrees at 78,000 ft (23,774 m) and Mach 3.17, passing over Haiphong. In just 12 minutes they had overflown Hanoi – then the most highly defended city on earth – with impunity, the jet's sensors recording dozens of high-value targets, before exiting hostile airspace in the vicinity of Dien Bien Phu.

Decelerating and descending over Thailand, the crew rendezvoused with several KC-135Q tankers and took on 80,000 lbs of JP-7 from two of them. With fuel in the tanks, Maj O'Malley quickly reached the SR-71's optimum speed and altitude and headed back over North Vietnam, before plotting a course for 'home-plate' – Kadena air base, on Okinawa.

It was whilst completing this leg of the mission that Maj Payne managed to successfully operate the aircraft's troublesome high resolution ground mapping radar – an action that later enabled USAF intelligence interpreters to establish the location of a large camouflaged supply area that was responsible for providing logistical support to North Vietnamese Army units pinning down US Marines at Khe Sanh. A follow-up B-52 raid was mounted on 7 April, obliterating the site in North Vietnam, and allowing the besieged troops at Khe Sanh to be relieved.

In recognition of the successful completion of this historic and significant flight, Majs O'Malley and Payne were each awarded the Distinguished Flying Cross (*Cover artwork by Gareth Hector*)

For Mia

First published in Great Britain in 2008 by Osprey Publishing
Midland House, West Way, Botley, Oxford, OX2 0PH
443 Park Avenue South, New York, NY, 10016, USA
E-mail; info@ospreypublishing.com

ISBN: 978 1 84603 319 3

Edited by Tony Holmes
Page design by Tony Truscott
Cover Artwork by Gareth Hector
Aircraft Profiles by Chris Davey
Line drawings by Mark Styling
Index by Michael Forder
Originated by PDQ Digital Media Solutions
Printed and bound in China through Bookbuilders

CONTENTS

OXCART AND TAGBOARD

Having just completed a 90-degree left turn that would align him with his next intelligence gathering objective, the pilot, cocooned in his full pressure suit, was busy recording time, altitude, speed and Exhaust Gas Temperature (EGT) details on his kneepad when he felt a dull thump. The aircraft jerked forward and a tremendous orange flash lit up both the cockpit and the sky.

It was 1 May 1960, and Central Intelligence Agency (CIA) Lockheed U-2C Article Number 360, flown by Francis Gary Powers, had just been hit by an SA-2 surface-to-air missile (SAM) during a deep penetration sortie of the USSR. What had been the United States' most successful, and politically sensitive, aerial intelligence gathering programme of the Cold War to date was about to be exposed to the world in spectacular fashion by a canny and jubilant President Nikita Khrushchev.

The subsonic U-2's growing vulnerability to developing Soviet SAM technologies had been recognised in the CIA several years prior to the shoot down, and studies had begun to find a replacement for the aircraft. Using the codename *Rainbow*, the Boston-based Scientific Engineering Institute (SEI), which was a CIA proprietary, concluded that when faced with such threats, platform survivability could be significantly enhanced by designing an aircraft with a small radar cross-section (RCS). It should also feature radar absorbent materials (RAM), which would further assist in reducing the aircraft's radar reflectivity. Harnessing these techniques to an aeroplane capable of flying at supersonic speeds at extreme altitudes would afford yet further protection against a successful interception.

In August 1957, *Rainbow's* findings were presented to the CIA's Special Assistant for Planning and Coordination, Richard M Bissell, and

Initially accorded the classified cryptonym *Aquatone*, the U-2 platform equipped with the Hycon Type B camera provided its CIA operators with exceptional high-resolution imagery of highly sensitive Soviet military establishments and hardware (*Lockheed*)

shortly thereafter they became enshrined in a CIA general operation requirement, specifically designed to produce a U-2 replacement. The project was given the secret codename *Gusto*, and John Parangosky was nominated as the CIA's project manager.

It was from Parangosky's office that the bureau head of Lockheed's Advanced Development Projects (ADP), Clarence L 'Kelly' Johnson, and Robert Whidmer of the Convair Division of General Dynamics were informed of the SEI's findings. However, due to security constraints, both were asked to submit designs without a formal contract or government funding. They agreed to this on the basis that funding would be forthcoming at 'the appropriate time'. Over the following 18 months, configurations were developed and refined, all at no expense to the CIA.

It was apparent to Bissell that *Gusto* would be both hi-tech and high risk for both competing companies. Furthermore, success in the venture was by no means guaranteed. The project would therefore require government funding to underwrite the financial liability, and this would inevitably mean that a number of high-ranking government officials would have to be briefed in order to secure the necessary monies.

Consequently, on 19 November 1957 Bissell reported the project to Deputy Secretary of Defense Donald A Quarles, who agreed that it should also be reported to the President's Board of Consultants on Foreign Intelligence Activities. In addition, Bissell established an evaluation panel, chaired by Edwin Land of the Polaroid Corporation, that consisted of eminent experts in their respective scientific disciplines.

On 25 November 1958, the Land Panel conducted a review of studies provided to it by the two competing design teams and decided that each company would be granted a year to refine its initial proposal and generate a definitive aircraft design. This decision was relayed to President Dwight Eisenhower, and he, together with the Killian Committee, reviewed both the *Gusto* programme and other design options. At the end of that meeting, the President agreed that funding would be made available from the CIA's special Contingency Reserve Fund for development of a tri-sonic reconnaissance platform.

Within Lockheed's ADP facility (known as the 'Skunk Works') at Burbank, in California, Johnson and programme manager Dick Boehme went into overdrive and studied no less than ten major design models designated A-3 to A-12. Within Lockheed, the high-flying U-2 had been referred to as 'Kelly's Angel'. The considerably enhanced performance capabilities of this latest creation in-the-making led to it being christened 'Archangel' – hence the letter 'A' in the prefix of each design.

On 20 August 1959, the final design submissions from both Lockheed and General Dynamics were delivered to the joint Department of Defense (DoD)/USAF/CIA selection panel. Despite the strikingly different external appearances of the two designs, their Mach 3.2 performance characteristics were extremely similar. Nine days later, Lockheed received official notification that its A-12 design had beaten General Dynamics' Kingfisher competitor, and on 3 September it received $4.5 million by way of an advanced feasibility contract. The programme was given the classified codename *Oxcart* at this time.

It is difficult to overstate the challenges that lay ahead for the design team. The best frontline fighter of the day at that time was the early

'century series' F-101 Voodoo. With the A-12, Lockheed had signed up to produce an aeroplane that would routinely operate at sustained speeds and altitudes that were twice as fast and twice as high as those achievable in the McDonnell interceptor. Kelly Johnson would later remark that virtually everything on the aircraft had to be invented from scratch.

Lockheed discovered that when flying above 80,000 ft, the ambient air temperature was at least -56 degrees Centigrade, and the atmospheric air pressure just 0.4 lbs per square inch. However, when cruising in afterburner at a speed of a mile every two seconds, airframe temperatures soared to between 245-565 degrees Centigrade. Sustained operation in this thermal thicket, therefore, meant the lavish use of advanced titanium alloys, which accounted for 85 per cent of the A-12's structural weight – the remaining 15 per cent was comprised of composite materials.

To power this awesome aircraft, Pratt & Whitney developed the JT11D-20 engine, which was designated the J58 by the US military. This powerplant had its origins in the JT9 – a single-spool, high pressure ratio turbojet rated at 26,000 lbs in afterburner that had been developed for an ill-fated US Navy project. Utilising a unique bleed bypass system developed by Pratt & Whitney's Robert Abernathy to solve problems associated with high compressor inlet temperatures (CIT), the J58 produced a maximum uninstalled afterburning thrust of 34,000 lbs under sea-level static conditions.

But the engine, remarkable as it was, was only one element of the power-producing story. The A-12 also boasted a unique, highly efficient, Air Inlet Control (AIC) system that supplemented thrust via three components – an asymmetric mixed-compression variable-geometry inlet, the J58 engine and a convergent/divergent blow-in door ejector nozzle. The AIC system was thereby able to regulate the massively varying internal airflow throughout the aircraft's entire flight envelope,

Also operated successfully by the USAF, the U-2's vulnerability to Soviet SA-2 surface-to-air missile attack was well understood by both Lockheed and the CIA long before the Francis Gary Powers incident on 1 May 1960 (*Lockheed*)

thus ensuring that both engines always received air at the correct velocity and pressure.

On 27 February 1962, the first A-12 (Article Number 121 and USAF 60-6924) arrived in two custom-built trailers at the nominated test base at Area 51, in the Nevada desert. Lockheed used a three-figure number, referred to as an Article Number, to identify individual airframes, and this was also used as a reference by the CIA. The USAF serial number, based on the fiscal year of order, bore no relationship to the Article Number, and since *Oxcart* was not an Air Force programme, Article Numbers will be the term of reference for A-12 aircraft used in this book.

By 24 April engine test runs, together with low and medium-speed taxi tests, had been successfully completed. Two days later, Lockheed Chief Test Pilot Lou Schalk took the A-12 aloft for the first time. However, due to significant development issues with the engine, it was not until 15 January 1963 that the first test flight of an A-12 powered by two J58s was completed – all flights up until then had been made utilising far less powerful J75 engines.

EARLY LOSS

Given the highly sophisticated nature of *Oxcart*, it is perhaps not surprising that success was not obtained without loss. The first A-12 to be written-off in an accident was aircraft 60-6926, Article Number 123, which crashed on 24 May 1963. After entering thick cloud, the aircraft fell into an inverted flat spin due to inadequate pitot tube provision, leading to a failure of the air data computer. Luckily, pilot Ken Collins ejected safely and the authorities were able to cover up the true identity of the crashed aircraft, claiming that it was a Republic F-105 Thunderchief.

On 20 July 1963, Article Number 121 became the first A-12 to reach Mach 3.0. Later, Lou Schalk would recall that it took 66 flights to push the speed envelope out from Mach 2.0 to Mach 3.2 – the aircraft's design

Lined-up sequentially, seven single-seat A-12s, AT-12 '927' (the two-seat trainer dubbed the 'Titanium Goose') and two YF-12As sit on the ramp at Groom Lake for a one-off photo-call in early 1963. In the foreground is '926', which became the first A-12 to be lost in an accident when it crashed on 24 May 1963. The third jet in the line-up ('928') was lost on 7 January 1967, while '929' was written-off on 28 December 1967 (*Lockheed*)

speed. A major obstacle to achieving this speed, and, therefore, operational readiness, was the need to resolve a phenomenon unique to the A-12 known as an 'un-start'.

The variable geometry air inlet maintained a pre-programmed ratio between dynamic pressure at the inlet cowl on one side of the inlet throat and the static duct pressure on the other side. Above 82,000 ft (24,994 m), the ambient air pressure is 0.4 psi (2.76 kPa), but the design of the intake duct enabled internal air pressures to reach 18 psi (124 kPa). This pressure differential generated an enormous pressure gradient, which in turn produced a similarly large forward thrust vector. In fact, at Mach cruise, this accounted for no less than 54 per cent of the total thrust being produced, with a further 29 per cent being generated by the ejector nozzles and the remaining 17 per cent coming from the J58 engines.

The performance of the air inlet was highly impressive until a disturbance in the airflow disrupted the all-important pressure balance. When such an incident occurred, the normal shock wave associated with supersonic flight was literally 'belched' forward from the inlet throat, causing an instant drop in the inlet pressure and a corresponding loss of thrust. With each engine positioned at mid-semi span, the shock wave departure manifested itself in a vicious yaw in the direction of the un-started engine.

Sometimes these incidents were so violent that crewmembers had their helmets slammed against the cockpit canopy framing. Recovery from an un-start involved an automatic, computer-sequenced inlet restart in an effort to recapture and reposition the shock wave. This took time and, until the advent of the Digital Automatic Flight Inlet Control System (DAFICS) in the late 1970s, invariably meant loss of speed and altitude – not an enviable position for the crew to find itself in if such an incident occurred during an operational mission over denied territory!

Like the preceding U-2 programme, *Oxcart's* reconnaissance-gathering flights would be flown by highly experienced USAF pilots that had volunteered to serve with the CIA on a suspended Air Force contract. The US government felt that it would be less politically embarrassing if a civilian were to trigger an international incident (as had been the case with Francis Gary Powers) rather than a member of the military, as this could be construed as an act of war by the USSR.

When the would-be A-12 pilots first saw the futuristic jet, they were keen to confer on it a nickname both worthy of its design and cognisant of Lockheed's penchant for christening their aircraft after celestial bodies. It was Jack Weeks that came up with Cygnus (the Swan), which was the name of a constellation in the Northern Celestial Hemisphere, lying between Pegasus and Draco, in the Milky Way. The name was particularly apt for the secretive *Oxcart* programme, because research astronomers believe that Cygnus may also contain one of the most mysterious of Nature's invisible bodies – a black hole.

Spurred on by the success of his A-12 design for the CIA, Kelly Johnson discussed the possibility of building an interceptor version for the USAF, which met with considerable customer interest. Yet further design possibilities became apparent to the Lockheed team, which worked up other potential Air Force proposals – the B-12 bomber, the RS-12 reconnaissance strike variant and the R-12 reconnaissance-only

In order to accommodate the Hughes AN/ASG-18 fire control system's 40-inch diameter radar scanning dish in the nose of the YF-12A, the aircraft's distinctive fuselage chines were cut back. The accompanying loss of longitudinal stability was rectified by fitting dorsal fins beneath each engine nacelle and a large folding ventral fin on the underside of the rear fuselage. Bearing the Air Force Systems Command crest on its fin, 60-6934 was the first of three YF-12 prototypes assembled by Lockheed (*Lockheed*)

The highly classified nature of *Oxcart* dictated that its designer genius, Kelly Johnson, could only pose for this officially released photo standing beside one of his less sensitive tri-sonic YF-12A fighters. This particular aircraft (60-6936) was the last of the fighter prototypes to be built (*Lockheed*)

platform. Key to this remarkable flexibility in the A-12 design was a realisation that the entire wing, engines and aft section could remain common to all variants. The difference would be in the forward fuselage section from a point identified as joint 715 (perpendicular to where the inboard wing section meets the fuselage).

A 'universal aircraft' common to three key Air Force disciplines could be of enormous benefit, offering huge unit cost savings by reducing construction and maintenance costs due to a high level of commonality of type throughout the inventory – not to mention, of course, the unprecedented financial windfall potentially on offer to Lockheed!

Three Mach 3 YF-12A fighters were built and tested under the classified codename *Kedlock*. And despite having demonstrated staggering capabilities in terms of both performance and the accuracy of the missile/fire control system, the F-12 programme was cancelled by then Secretary of Defense Robert McNamara on 1 February 1968.

Neither the B-12 nor RS-12 progressed beyond the mock-up stage, as several key senators and senior Air Force officers voiced concern that one manufacturer should not have such a wide-ranging monopoly on the production of frontline types. It is also true to say that several of these individuals were strong advocates of what would have been rival designs to the Lockheed proposals – the ill-fated North American XB-70 Valkyrie bomber was one such aircraft. The R-12 design, however, was an entirely different issue, and it was destined to become the legendary SR-71.

TAGBOARD

In early 1962, a meeting took place between Kelly Johnson and Dr Eugene Fubini of the Department of Defense's Office of Research and Engineering. During the discussion, the Lockheed designer was asked if it would be possible to develop a small-scale version of the A-12 that could be droned, carry a reasonable reconnaissance payload and possess similar performance characteristics to those anticipated for the full-sized, manned A-12. The US government was keen to avoid the political fall-out that followed the U-2/Powers shoot-down, and to prevent American citizens from falling into the hands of the Soviet authorities.

On 10 October 1962, Kelly Johnson received authorisation from the CIA to examine whether a drone could be carried by an A-12. Two weeks later, a 'Skunk Works' team consisting of Kelly Johnson, Ben Rich and Rus Daniel met

Article Number 132 (60-6938) was the twelfth A-12 constructed by Lockheed. It had completed 197 flights totalling 369.9 hours by the time it was withdrawn from service in mid-1968 following the termination of the *Oxcart* programme. Stored at Lockheed's Plant 42 in Palmdale for 20 years, the aircraft has been on display in the USS *Alabama* Battleship Memorial Park in Mobile, Alabama, since the late 1980s. The A-12 was badly damaged during Hurricane *Katrina* in September 2005 (*USAF*)

representatives from Marquardt to discuss ramjet propulsion system options. Progress was rapid, and on 7 December a full-scale mock up of the craft (which was referred to within the 'Skunk Works' as the Q-12) was completed.

Still to receive mission specifications from the CIA, Lockheed worked on producing a vehicle that was fitted with a 425-lb Hycon camera system capable of achieving a photographic resolution of six inches from operating altitude. The drone would have a range of 3000 nautical miles and be powered by a single Marquardt RJ-43-MA-11 ramjet. By October 1963, the overall configuration for the Q-12, and its launch platform – two purpose-built, modified A-12s – were nearing completion. Codenamed *Tagboard*, the designation of both elements was also changed, with the carrier vehicle becoming the M-21 ('M' standing for 'Mother') and the Q-12 the D-21 ('D' standing for 'Daughter').

The 11,000-lb D-21 was supported on the M-21 by a single, dorsally mounted, pylon. Upon reaching launch point, the mothership's pilot maintained Mach 3.12 and initiated a 0.9G push over. Once released by the Launch Control Officer (LCO), who was sitting in what was the 'Q-bay' (sensor bay) in other A-12s, the D-21 flew its sortie independently utilising an autopilot system that was integrated into a Minneapolis-Honeywell inertial navigation system (INS). This enabled the D-21 to fly a pre-programmed flight profile, execute turns and switch the camera on/off at appropriate points in the mission so as to perform the perfect photo-reconnaissance sortie.

Having completed its camera run, the drone's INS system then sent signals to the autopilot system to descend to a predetermined 'feet wet' film collection point. The entire palletised unit, containing INS, camera and film, was then ejected at 60,000 ft and Mach 1.67 and parachuted towards the ocean. As the drone continued its descent, it was destroyed by a barometrically activated explosive charge. Meanwhile, air retrieval of the palletised unit was executed by a JC-130B Hercules.

Project *Tagboard* was a direct result of the Francis Gary Powers shoot-down. Launched at Mach 3 from a modified A-12, the tri-sonic pilotless D-21 drone was to prove both expensive and ultimately unreliable (*USAF*)

On 12 August 1964, the first M-21 was despatched to Groom Lake. Four months later, on 22 December, the first D-21/M-21 combination flight took place, with Bill Park at the controls. Troubles soon beset *Tagboard*, however, and it was not until 5 March 1965 that

One of two *Tagboard* M-21s, this example (Article Number 135) was written-off on 30 July 1966 following collision with its drone during the separation procedure. Ray Torrick, the Launch Control Officer seated in the back of the mothership, drowned in the subsequent 'feet-wet' parachute landing off the coast of California (*Lockheed*)

Senior Bowl was a later attempt to utilise the D-21 drone following cancellation of *Tagboard*. Launched from a modified B-52H, the drone was accelerated to speed and altitude by a rocket booster, which then separated, allowing the platform's ramjet to takeover. This programme also proved unreliable, and was cancelled on 23 July 1971 after just four operational sorties, all of which failed to successfully deliver imagery (*Lockheed*)

the first successful D-21 launch was accomplished. The second launch, on 27 April, saw the drone reach Mach 3.3 at 90,000 ft and fly for 1200 nautical miles, holding its course to within half-a-mile throughout. The flight ended when a hydraulic pump burned out and the D-21 crashed.

Despite ongoing development problems, the USAF remained committed to the drone, and on 29 April 1966 a second batch of D-21s was ordered. Six weeks later, on 16 June, a third successful launch was at last made, with the D-21 flying 1600 miles and completing all tasks on the flight card, bar the ejection of the all important camera pallet. The fourth, and final, D-21 sortie from the M-21 occurred on 30 July 1966, and it ended in disaster when the drone collided with 60-6941 moments after achieving launch separation. The impact caused the mother aircraft to pitch up so violently that the fuselage fore-body broke off. Both Bill Park and his LCO, Ray Torick, successfully ejected and made a 'feet wet' landing, but Torick's pressure suit filled with water and he drowned before he could be rescued. Bill Park spent an hour in the ocean prior to being recovered by a US Navy vessel.

In the wake of this accident, the D-21 was grounded for a year whilst a new launch system was developed under the codename *Senior Bowl*. The drone would now be launched from the underwing pylons of two modified B-52Hs of the 4200th Test Wing, based at Beale AFB in California. Upon launch, the D-21B was accelerated to Mach 3.3 and 80,000 ft by a solid propellant rocket developed by the Lockheed Propulsion Company of Redlands, California. On achieving cruise speed and altitude, the booster was jettisoned and the drone's flight continued as described earlier under the power of the RJ-43-MA-11 ramjet.

The first attempt at launching a D-21B from a B-52 was made on 6 November 1967, and this proved unsuccessful. Following three more attempts, the drone finally separated correctly in flight on 16 June 1968. Between 9 November 1969 and 20 March 1971, four operational drone flights were made over communist China. To maintain tight security, the B-52, hauling its unique payload, left Beale at night and headed westwards across the Pacific to Guam. The flight resumed just before dawn the next day, when the bomber departed Guam for the launch point. Upon vehicle separation, the B-52 returned to Guam, while the D-21 embarked upon its pre-programmed daytime reconnaissance run.

Achieving only limited success, *Senior Bowl* was cancelled on 15 July 1971.

BLACK SHIELD

On 27 January 1965, the first in a series of long-range, high-speed, high-altitude proving flights, codenamed *Silver Javelin*, occurred. Article Number 129 completed the 2580-nautical mile flight in just one hour and forty minutes, one hour and fifteen minutes of which was spent at speeds in excess of Mach 3.1. Cruising altitudes of between 75,600 ft and 80,000 ft were also achieved.

Later that year, on 18 March 1965, the heads of both the CIA and DoD agreed to take preparatory steps towards operating the A-12 over communist China. By year-end, all the Agency's project pilots were Mach 3 qualified. Yet despite this near-state of readiness, political sensitivities surrounding the overflight conundrum ensured that *Oxcart* would never conduct sorties over the USSR or China. Where then was this multi-million dollar national security asset to earn its keep? One possible short-term answer appeared to be in a classified project, codenamed *Upwind*.

In 1964, a KH-4 Corona space photo-reconnaissance satellite shot imagery of what some analysts believed was an anti-ballistic missile site in the Estonian capital, Tallinn. A highly classified proposal codenamed Project *Scope Logic* (with the classified cryptonym Project *Upwind*) envisaged conducting a composite mission, wherein an A-12 would fly from the US into the Baltic Sea and rendezvous with a U-2 – the latter configured to gather electronic intelligence (ELINT). The A-12 would then proceed north of Norway, before swinging back south along the Soviet-Finnish border. Prior to reaching Leningrad, the pilot would head west-southwest down the Baltic Sea, skirting the coasts of Estonia, Latvia, Lithuania, Poland and East Germany, before heading west to the US.

The 11,000-mile flight would take eight hours and forty minutes to complete, and the A-12 would require four aerial refuellings. Although not violating Soviet airspace, it was hoped that the high speed, high altitude target would provoke Soviet radar operators into activating the Tallinn system. The A-12, with its Type 1 camera, would secure high-resolution imagery of the anti-ballistic missile site, while the more vulnerable U-2 would stand off beyond SA-2 range, recording the radar's signal characteristics. Although both Agency and DoD officials supported the proposal, Secretary of State Dean Rusk was strongly opposed to it, and the influential, and secretive, '303 Committee' (which oversaw covert activities) never forwarded the proposal to President Lyndon Johnson for his approval.

Another possible area of operations for *Oxcart* was Cuba. By early 1964, Project headquarters had already begun planning for possible 'contingency overflights' under a programme codenamed *Skylark*. Four of the thirteen A-12s now at Area 51 were initially designated as primary *Skylark* aircraft, namely Article Numbers 125, 127, 128 and 132, and they were later supplemented by aircraft 129 and 131 following the installation of further modifications. However, during a meeting on 15 September between Agency and government officials, a consensus concerning

In spite of its radical external appearance and awesome capabilities, in the cockpit the A-12 was generally conventional, as this 8 November 1965 shot taken by Lockheed technicians illustrates (*Lockheed*)

platform vulnerability over the skies of Cuba could not be reached, so it was agreed that further studies should be undertaken.

On 5 August 1965, the Director of the National Security Agency, Gen Marshall S Carter, directed that *Skylark* was to achieve emergency operational readiness by 5 November. Should security considerations dictate, any contingency sorties would have to be executed below the optimum capability of the A-12 (nearer to Mach 2.8). In order to meet this tight timeframe, the aircraft would have to be deployed without their full electronic countermeasures (ECM) suite.

Despite having little time to prepare the jets, a limited capability was ready on the date prescribed by Gen Carter. In the event, the Cuban contingencies were never implemented, for on 15 September 1966, the '303 Committee' voted not to commit *Oxcart* to Cuban reconnaissance missions on the basis that they could be interpreted as being provocative, thus disturbing the prevailing political calm. Instead, a more critical situation had by now developed in Southeast Asia, and this took priority.

On 22 March 1965, Brig Gen Jack Ledford briefed Deputy Secretary of Defense Cyrus Vance on project *Black Shield* – the planned deployment of *Oxcart* to the Japanese island of Okinawa in response to the increased SA-2 threat that was now being faced by U-2 and Firebee drone reconnaissance assets that were performing overflights of communist China. Such missions would obviously have to be approved by the President himself, but Secretary Vance was willing to make $3.7 million available to construct support facilities at Kadena air base – these were to be ready by the autumn of 1965.

On 3 June 1965, Secretary McNamara consulted with the Under Secretary of the Air Force on the build-up of SA-2 missile sites around Hanoi, and the possibility of substituting A-12s for the vulnerable U-2s that were flying reconnaissance overflights of the North Vietnamese capital. He was informed that *Black Shield* could operate over Vietnam as soon as adequate aircraft performance was validated.

On 20 November 1965, the final stage of the *Silver Javelin* validation process was completed when a maximum-endurance flight of six hours and twenty minutes was achieved, during which time the A-12 demonstrated sustained speeds above Mach 3.2 at altitudes approaching 90,000 ft. Four A-12s were selected for *Black Shield* operations, with Kelly Johnson taking personal responsibility for ensuring that the aircraft were completely 'squawk-free'.

The '303 Committee' received a formal proposal to deploy *Oxcart* operations to the Far East on 2 December 1965. The proposal was quickly rejected, but the committee agreed that all steps should be taken to develop a quick-reaction capability for deploying the A-12 system within a 21-day period anytime after 1 January 1966.

Throughout 1966, numerous requests were made to the committee to implement the *Black Shield* Operations Order, but they were all turned down. Crew training and testing continued, however, and the amount of time it would take to deploy the A-12s was further reduced from 21 to 11 days. To further underwrite the aircraft's capability to carry out long-range reconnaissance missions, Bill Park completed a non-stop 10,200-mile flight in just over six hours on 21 December 1966.

However, just 15 days after Park's proof-of-range flight, tragedy struck the programme with the crash of yet another jet, and this time the incident claimed the life of pilot Walt Ray. Getting airborne from Area 51 at 1150 hrs (local) on 5 January 1967, and using his personal call sign 'Dutch 45', Walt was just completing the last 30 minutes of a routine training and test sortie when he reported that his fuel consumption was running abnormally high. At 1522 hrs he radioed that he was down to 7500 lbs, and commented 'I don't know where it's gone'.

Thirty minutes later, during his descent near Hanksville, in Utah, he reported that he was low on fuel, and just one minute later declared an emergency. At 1556 hrs he radioed that he was 130 miles out, with just 4000 lbs of fuel left, and he was losing this at an excessive rate. Five minutes later he reported that the fuel low-pressure lights had illuminated, then, after 30 seconds, he stated that the engines were flaming out. At 1603 hrs Walt made his final radio call, reporting that both engines had flamed out and that he was ejecting. Article Number 125 (60-6928) had run out of fuel just 70 miles short of Area 51.

After 'gliding' to a lower altitude, and executing a controlled bale out, Walt could not separate his parachute from the ejection seat and was killed when he hit the ground. It was a devastating loss of both an outstanding pilot and an extremely popular member of the programme.

CONFLICT ESCALATION

In May 1967, the National Security Council received intelligence reports that North Vietnam was about to receive surface-to-surface ballistic missiles. Such a serious escalation of the conflict would require hard evidence to substantiate reports obtained through clandestine means.

President Johnson was briefed on the threat, and Director of Central Intelligence (DCI) Richard Helms of the CIA again proposed that the '303 Committee' authorise deployment of *Oxcart*, as it was ideally equipped to undertake such a surveillance task thanks to its superior performance when compared with U-2s and pilotless drones. The A-12 was also equipped with a better camera. President Johnson approved the plan, and in mid-May an airlift began to establish *Black Shield* at Kadena.

Heavily involved in the training effort for CIA pilots assigned to *Oxcart*, 60-6928 was the fifth A-12 constructed by Lockheed. Having completed 202 flights, it was lost on 5 January 1967 when a massive leak caused it to run out of fuel during a Groom Lake training mission. Pilot Walt Ray successfully ejected, but he was killed when when he failed to separate from his ejection seat (*Lockheed*)

Mele Vojvodich positioned the first A-12 from Area 51 to Kadena air base on 22 May 1967. He subsequently flew the same aircraft (Article Number 131) on *Black Shield*'s debut operational mission on 31 May 1967. Vojvodich is seen here wearing a David Clark S-901 full-pressure flight suit – the 'yellow box' is a portable oxygen and environmental control unit (*CIA*)

The first A-12 pilot to deploy was Mele Vojvodich, who departed Area 51 in Article Number 131 (60-6937) at 0800 hrs on 22 May 1967. He arrived at Kadena after three aerial refuellings and an uneventful flight that lasted for just over six hours – were it not for the deployment's secrecy, this mission could have been recognised for having set a new transpacific speed record. Two days later Jack Layton arrived on the island in Article Number 127 (60-6930), and on 26 May Jack Weeks departed Area 51 in Article Number 129 (60-6932). However, due to INS and radio problems, he was forced to divert to Wake Island. An *Oxcart* maintenance team arrived in a KC-135 from Okinawa the next day, after which Jack was able to complete the final 'hop' to Kadena.

With all three aircraft now safely deployed, the detachment was declared ready for operations on 29 May. Following a weather reconnaissance flight the following day, it was determined that conditions over North Vietnam were ideal for an *Oxcart* photo-run.

Project Headquarters in Washington, DC then placed *Black Shield* on alert for its first ever operational mission. Avionics specialists checked various systems and sensors, and at 1600 hrs Vojvodich and back-up pilot Layton attended a mission-alert briefing that included such details as the projected take-off and landing times, routes to and from the target and a full intelligence briefing of the area to be overflown. At 2200 hrs (12 hours before planned take-of time), a review of the weather confirmed that the mission was still on, so the pilots went to bed to ensure that they got a full eight hours of 'crew rest'.

They awoke on the morning of the 31st to torrential rain – a new phenomenon for 'desert dwelling' A-12s and their crews! The two pilots ate breakfast, dressed and proceeded to prepare for the mission, despite local rain. Since meteorological conditions over 'the collection area' were good, at 0800 hrs Kadena received a final clearance

Modified USAF KC-135Q tankers of the 903rd Air Refueling Squadron, based at Beale AFB, provided essential tanker support for *Oxcart*. The aircraft were equipped with specialist communications equipment to fulfil their role (*CIA*)

This extremely rare shot of a *Black Shield* A-12 getting airborne from Kadena was copied from a 16 mm ciné film taken by a member of the *Oxcart* team. Note the wing vortices generated as a consequence of the high humidity (*CIA*)

A second image taken from the same 16 mm ciné film of a *Black Shield* A-12 flying out of Kadena in 1967 (*CIA*)

from Washington, DC that *Black Shield* flight BSX001 was definitely 'On'. The rain, however, continued unabated, casting serious doubts over the launch of the A-12. The pilot had the final say in the matter since conditions were within USAF take-off limits. Vojvodich, who was well aware of the pressure on the programme to 'deliver', elected to launch.

After brief medical checks, he and Jack Layton both donned their S-901 full pressure suits and began breathing 100 per cent pure oxygen to purge their bodies of potentially harmful nitrogen. By taxi-time, the rain was falling so heavily that a staff car had to lead Vojvodich from the hangar to the end of the main runway. After lining up for what would be the first instrument-guided take-off performed by an A-12, on cue, the pilot engaged both afterburners and accelerated '131' rapidly down the runway, disappearing into the rain and then climbing upward through the drenching clouds.

A few minutes later, Vojvodich burst through the cloud and flew the jet up to 25,000 ft, where he topped-off its tanks from a waiting KC-135. With the refuelling complete, he disconnected from the tanker's boom and accelerated to operational speed. The A-12 steadily climbed to its optimum altitude while building up its speed, the pilot informing Kadena ('home-plate') that the aircraft's systems were functioning correctly. The back-up services of Jack Layton would not be required on this mission.

Vojvodich penetrated hostile airspace at 80,000 ft while flying at a speed of Mach 3.2, the A-12 performing a so-called 'front door' entry over Haiphong and then continuing to Hanoi, before exiting North Vietnam near Dien Bien Phu. A second air refuelling took place over Thailand, followed by another climb to speed and altitude and a second penetration of North Vietnamese airspace near the Demilitarised Zone (DMZ), after which Vojvodich recovered the aircraft at Kadena – but not before he had made three instrument approaches in driving rain. The flight had lasted three hours and forty minutes.

The 'photo-take' was downloaded and sent by a special courier aircraft to the Eastman Kodak plant in Rochester, New York, for processing, where it was discovered that the Type 1 camera had performed flawlessly. Ten priority target categories, including 70 of the 190 known SAM sites in the area, had been successfully photographed.

During the first three months of *Black Shield* operations, nine missions were successfully completed, and by mid-July *Oxcart* over-flights had determined with a high degree of confidence that there were no surface-to-surface missiles in North Vietnam. These sorties had proven to be invaluable, as they provided timely information to those planning strike missions as to what SA-2 sites were occupied, as well as high quality bomb damage assessment (BDA) imagery. The latter was essential when it came to determining just how effective the strike had been. From September through to the end of December 1967, the three *Black Shield* A-12s completed 13 operational missions – the highest period of activity was reached in October, when seven sorties were flown.

During sortie number BX6732 on 28 October 1967, flown by Denny Sullivan, the pilot received indications on his Radar Homing Warning Receiver (RHWR) of almost continuous radar activity focused on his A-12 whilst both inbound and outbound over North Vietnam. This culminated in the launch of a single SA-2. Two days later, whilst flying Article Number 129 during sortie BX6734, Sullivan was again flying high over North Vietnam when two SAM sites tracked him on his first pass. On his second run, whilst approaching Hanoi from the east, he again noted that he was being tracked on radar, then, over the next few minutes, he counted no less than eight SA-2 detonations in 'the general area, though none were particularly close'. This was the first occasion that the North Vietnamese had employed a salvo launch technique.

After recovering the aircraft back at Kadena without further incident, a post flight inspection revealed that a tiny piece of shrapnel had penetrated the lower wing fillet of his aircraft and become lodged against the support structure of the wing tank – history would prove this to be the only enemy damage inflicted on an A-12 or SR-71.

Oxcart missions BX6737 and BX6738 both utilised Article Number 131, and were flown by Mel Vojvodich on 8 December 1967 and Jack Layton two days later. For the first time, the 'collection area' was Cambodia, and the 'target' was communist troop concentrations. During the four-hour sortie on the 8th, cloud cover obscured four of the seven special search areas in the extreme northeast of Cambodia, including both primary targets. Limited troop activity was detected, however, where the Tonle San River crosses the Cambodia/Laos border, as was the re-grading of the natural surface runway at Ban Pania airfield.

In contrast, the virtually cloud-free conditions experienced by Jack Layton enabled his Type 1 camera to gather valuable photography on all seven priority search areas. Despite the weather, this mission was not without its problems. Layton recalled that a fault with the INS caused the aircraft to overshoot the planned track during turns, causing him to 'penetrate the bamboo curtain'. After turning south, and getting back on an approximate course toward *Scope Pearl* (his KC-135Qs) over Thailand, Layton then had difficulty finding the tankers due to low cloud and poor visibility;

'I got the aircraft up in a bank to search for the tankers, but the visibility from an A-12 is very poor – you can look down and see the ground, but you can't look inside the turn because of the canopy roof. I'd just about reached the point where I was about to divert to Takhli due to a lack of fuel when I finally saw the tankers. We got together, and I was able to complete the mission, even though the INS wasn't working.'

TARGET NORTH KOREA

During 1967, a total of 41 A-12 missions were alerted, of which 22 were actually granted approval for flight. Between 1 January and 31 March 1968, 17 missions were alerted, of which seven were flown – four over North Vietnam and three over North Korea.

In a CIA document classified Top Secret, the rationale was outlined for *Oxcart* reconnaissance missions against North Korea. It stated that the 'belligerent pronouncements by the communist country's civil and military leaders, and an increase in the number and expanded scope of North Korean probes along the DMZ, coupled with their efforts to establish the structure for guerrilla operations in the Republic, had established a critical requirement for accurate intelligence'.

The document also noted that satellite photo missions had not provided adequate imagery of North Korea to satisfy the intelligence requirement, and that ground collection of such photography was becoming increasingly difficult. This ultimately meant that it had become virtually impossible to accurately estimate the capabilities of the North Korean military, and the intentions of its communist leadership.

The CIA continued that the operational concept could now be accomplished on a 24-hour alert basis using operational *Black Shield* assets in place at Kadena without coverage degradation of targets in North Vietnam. Three passes traversing the target areas, east to west or west to east, could be accomplished utilising two aerial refuellings, or two passes of similar orientation could be executed with a single aerial refuelling.

On a footnote at the bottom of an attached sample route map, the Agency added that photographic resolution would be in the order of one to three-and-a-half feet, and that two eastbound passes and one westbound pass over North Korea would take a total of just 17 minutes to complete. Despite this, the US State Department initially vetoed the plan. This was soon to change, however, in the wake of the *Pueblo* incident.

On 5 January 1968, Auxiliary General Environmental Research Ship USS *Pueblo* (AGER-2) sailed as ordered, unprotected, on its maiden voyage to 'sample the electronic environment off the east coast of North Korea'. Onboard were a crew of six officers, two civilians and 75 enlisted men. Just 18 days later, during the night of 23 January, the ship's radio operator managed to get off an emergency signal. 'We Need Help! We are Holding Emergency Destruction! We Need Support! SOS. SOS. SOS. Please Send Assistance! SOS. SOS. SOS. We Are Being Boarded!' The last sentence clearly stated what was happening aboard the belea-

This map shows the routes flown by Frank Murray during his three passes over North Korea in A-12 Article Number 127 on 19 February 1968. The North Koreans were unaware that they had been overflown until they were informed about the flight by neighbouring China. Pass 1 took the A-12 directly over Wonsan harbour, where USS *Pueblo* (AGER-2) was being held

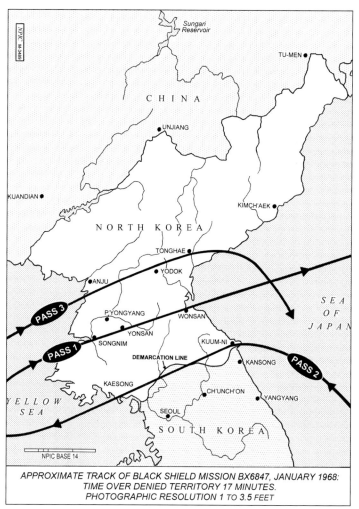

APPROXIMATE TRACK OF BLACK SHIELD MISSION BX6847, JANUARY 1968:
TIME OVER DENIED TERRITORY 17 MINUTES.
PHOTOGRAPHIC RESOLUTION 1 TO 3.5 FEET

guered vessel, and with one sailor dead and the rest of the crew captured, the year-long nightmare for Cdr Lloyd Bucher and his crew was just beginning.

In response to this potentially explosive international incident, President Johnson summoned his top advisors to a meeting at the White House the very next day (24 January) to plan a response and agree a course of action. Several hours later, DCI Richard Helms despatched a top-secret memo to Special Assistant to the President Walt Rostow, Secretary of Defense Robert McNamara, Under Secretary of State Nicholas Katzenbach, Deputy Secretary of Defense Paul Nitze and Chairman of the Joint Chiefs of Staff (JCS) Gen Earle Wheeler. In it, Helms referred to the earlier meeting, and confirmed that he was 'alerting an *Oxcart* mission for photo-reconnaissance of North Korea'.

The memo also confirmed that, 'The *Oxcart* mission has been alerted to take-off on 25 January at 2100 EST (1100/26 January) and return four-and-a-half hours later. The film will be off-loaded immediately and airlifted to Eastman Kodak, Rochester, New York, to arrive at approximately 0430 EST on 27 January. The processed film will be delivered immediately to the National Photographic Interpretation Center, with an arrival time of 1440 EST on 28 January'.

Point Three in the memo noted, 'The weather forecast for this mission indicates Category II (25 per cent or less cloud cover) weather conditions for the target area'. Finally Point Four confirmed that, 'No additional resources or support over and above those normally used on *Oxcart* North Vietnam operational sorties will be required for this mission'.

The draft CIA plan to overfly North Korea was about to be implemented in full, and three A-12 sorties would be flown as a consequence of the capture of the *Pueblo*. The first of these was BX6847 on 26 January (just 24 hours after the ship's capture), undertaken by Jack Weeks in Article Number 131. Equipped with Pin Peg, Mad Moth, Blue Dog II and System VI ECM defences, as well as a Type 1 camera, the A-12 located the *Pueblo* in Wonson Bay. And despite the right engine inlet unstarting on the third pass, Weeks' four-hour sortie was a huge success, helped by the fact that 90 per cent of North Korea was cloud-free.

A recently declassified critique of the mission noted that 71 of 84 programmed targets were covered, together with one surface-to-surface missile site, 81 of the 126 Committee on Imagery Requirements and Exploitation targets, 13 SAM sites (of which 12 were occupied) and 752 bonus targets. The report concluded that BX6847 'obtained good baseline coverage of most of North Korea's armed forces, as well as large portions of the transportation system and industrial base' – testament indeed to *Oxcart's* outstanding capabilities.

Despite the success of BX6847, US State Department officials were extremely wary of endorsing a second mission over North Korea after the

USS *Pueblo* (AGER-2) is seen here sailing off the coast of San Diego in October 1967, several months prior to inadvertently becoming the centre of a major international incident between North Korea and the United States. An 850-ton environmental research ship, *Pueblo* was built at Kewaunee, Wisconsin, in 1944 as the US Army cargo ship FP-344. Transferred to the US Navy in April 1966 and renamed *Pueblo*, it was initially designated a light cargo ship. Following conversion into a research ship, the vessel was recommissioned in May 1967. Completing training operations off California in November 1967, *Pueblo* headed for the Far East to undertake electronic intelligence collection and other duties (*US Navy*)

Pueblo and two North Korean torpedo boats were captured on film by the Type 1 camera mounted in Jack Weeks' A-12 during *Black Shield* mission BX6847 (*National Archive via Tim Brown*)

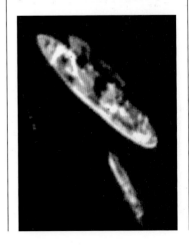

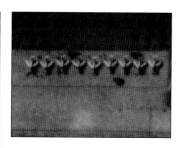

This photograph of one of the hardstands at Hwangiu air base reveals nine MiG-17 'Fresco' fighters – they posed no threat to *Oxcart* (*National Archive via Tim Brown*)

Another shot obtained by Jack Weeks during his overflight of North Korea on 26 January 1968. In addition to *Pueblo*, several airfields were also photographed, including this one at Hwangiu (*National Archive via Tim Brown*)

A more plausible threat to BX6847 were SA-2 sites, of which 12 of the 13 in North Korea in January 1968 were photographed by Jack Weeks (*National Archive via Tim Brown*)

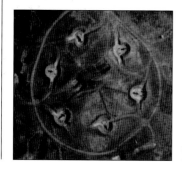

Pueblo event. The memories of the 1960 U-2/Powers incident still dominated decision making in Washington, DC. It was not until the CIA's USAF liaison officer Brig Gen Paul Baclais had briefed Secretary of State Dean Rusk on the mission objectives, and assured him that the A-12 would only be in North Korean airspace for seven minutes (the time taken to make two passes or 'photo lines'), that the State Department gave its blessing. The 3 hr 39 min sortie, designated BX6853, was flown by Frank Murray in Article Number 127 on 19 February 1968.

Equipped with the same sensors as '131', the A-12 found that 88 per cent of the programmed targets were cloud free, but the *Pueblo* was not. The vessel remained hidden from '127's' prying Type 1 camera.

On 6 May 1968, Jack Layton launched in Article Number 127 on sortie BX6858 and headed out on *Oxcart's* third mission to North Korea. Unbeknownst to him at the time, his sortie would prove to be the final operational flight of the A-12 programme. The reconnaissance 'take' was disappointing in comparison with the two earlier missions, as 50 per cent of the programmed targets suffered degradation from cloud and haze. Then, on the high-speed flight back to Kadena, 'milky white fingers' began slowly clawing their way across the front of the left windshield panel.

Having already experienced this 'white-out' phenomenon to a lesser degree during a stateside training sortie, Layton was fully aware of the cause of the problem. Frictional heating of the windscreen had turned the glue between its glass laminations viscous, leaving the windshield panel completely opaque. Proceeding on instruments all the way to landing, Layton completed a successful ground-directed radar approach and made a safe recovery back at Kadena.

Although the procurement of such intelligence information was not of direct benefit to Cdr Bucher and his crew, who were beaten and not released by their North Korean captors until 23 December 1968, such a 'hot-spot quick-look' capability was considered an early and important achievement of the *Oxcart* programme. These sorties demonstrated the validity of manned reconnaissance vehicles, and their ability to respond with minimal lead times to international incidents of political and military importance. At the same time, the incident brought an end to the US Navy's sea-borne foray into the world of signals intelligence trawling, as the two remaining AGERs were scrapped soon after *Pueblo's* seizure.

OXCART CLOSE-DOWN

It seems almost unbelievable that during the very month *Oxcart* was finally declared operational (November 1965), and before the programme had had the opportunity of fully vindicating itself, moves were already afoot to close it down. The Bureau of the Budget (BoB), questioned the necessity and cost of funding both the covert CIA *Oxcart* and 'overt' USAF *Senior Crown* SR-71 programmes. Its writer proposed several less costly alternatives, recommending that the A-12s be phased out by September 1966 and that all further procurement of SR-71s should stop. Copies of the memorandum were circulated within the DoD and the CIA, together with the suggestion that they explore the alternatives set out in the paper.

Since the SR-71 was not scheduled to become operational until September 1966, the Secretary of Defense quite rightly declined to accept the proposal. In July 1966, BoB officials suggested that a tri-agency study group be set up to again establish ways of reducing the costs of the two programmes. After the study was completed, a meeting was convened on 12 December 1966 and a vote was taken, during which three of the four votes cast were in favour of terminating the *Oxcart* fleet in January 1968 (assuming an operational readiness date of September 1967 for the SR-71), and assigning all missions to the SR-71 fleet.

The BoB's memorandum was transmitted to President Johnson four days later, despite protestations from the CIA's Richard Helms, who was the sole dissenting voice in the vote. On 28 December Johnson accepted the BoB's recommendations and directed that the *Oxcart* programme be terminated by 1 January 1968. However, as the war in Vietnam escalated and the results of *Black Shield's* outstanding work became apparent to a privileged few, the wisdom of the earlier phase-out decision was called into question. As a result, the run-down lagged and the question was re-opened.

A new feasibility and cost study of *Oxcart* was completed in the spring of 1968, and despite the continuing objections raised by Richard Helms, the original decision to terminate the programme was reaffirmed on 16 May 1968 by the Secretary of Defense. This decision was further endorsed by President Johnson five days later during his weekly luncheon with his principal advisors.

Project officials decided that 8 June 1968 would be the earliest date to begin the redeployment from Kadena back to the US. During the intervening period, sorties would be restricted to those essential for maintaining flight safety and pilot proficiency. Meanwhile, those aircraft back at Area 51 were to be flown to Palmdale and placed in storage by 7 June. At Kadena, preparations were being made for the A-12 ferry flights back to the US. Mission sensors were downloaded for the final time, and low-time/high-performance engines were replaced with less highly-tuned units. Functional Check Flights (FCFs) were also flown to confirm each aircraft's readiness for the transpacific ferry flights.

On 4 June, Jack Weeks left Kadena in '129' with the intention of conducting an FCF. He completed a 34,000-lb fuel on-load from the tanker, accelerated and climbed away – that was the last anyone ever saw of either the pilot or his aircraft. Forty-two minutes into the flight, the Birdwatcher sensor system in the A-12 transmitted a signal to Kadena, indicating that the starboard engine EGT was in excess of 860 degrees. Twenty-two seconds later, Birdwatcher detected that fuel-flow to the same engine was less than 7500 lbs per hour. Just eight more short seconds would pass before a third, and final, transmission was received from '129's' Birdwatcher. Repeating the earlier information, this time,

Jack Weeks was an extremely professional pilot, and popular member of the 1129th Special Activities Squadron. His death whilst conducting an FCF in Article Number 129 on 5 June 1968 was a bitter blow to a programme that had already been cancelled (*CIA*)

Lockheed Tech Rep Mel Rushing managed to 'weave' all the surviving A-12s into a hangar at Palmdale following the shutdown of *Oxcart* in mid-1968. Note the bogus red serial applied to either Article number 127 or 131 – the surviving *Black Shield* A-12s (*Lockheed*)

The coveted CIA Intelligence Star for Valour (*Dennis Sullivan*)

On 26 June 1968, in recognition of their outstanding service to their country, the surviving *Oxcart* pilots were presented with the CIA Intelligence Star for Valour by Vice Adm Rufus Taylor (Deputy Director of the CIA). These men are, from left to right, Mele Vojvodich (partially in shot) Dennis Sullivan, Rear Adm Taylor, Jack Layton, Ken Collins and Frank Murray (*CIA via Frank Murray*)

however, it ominously included data indicating that the aircraft was now at, or below, 68,500 ft.

From this limited evidence, it is reasonable to conclude that some kind of malfunction with the right engine involving an over-temperature and low fuel flow had somehow contributed to what appears to have been a catastrophic in-flight failure and subsequent aircraft break-up. Not a trace of wreckage was ever found. It was particularly ironic, and an especially cruel twist of fate, to lose such a highly competent and professional pilot on one of the very last flights in the *Oxcart* programme.

During early June 1968, the two remaining A-12s on Okinawa (Article Numbers 127 and 131) were ferried back to Area 51, before being sent to Palmdale. On reaching the Lockheed plant, company maintenance technicians drained all fuel and hydraulic lines, and Mel Rushing skilfully 'interwove' all nine remaining *Oxcart* aircraft into a tightly-regimented, sardine-like parking array in a corner of one of the large hangers, where they remained for more than 20 years before being dispersed to museums.

On 26 June 1968, Deputy Director of the CIA Vice Adm Rufus Taylor presided over a ceremony at Area 51 where he presented the CIA Intelligence Star for Valour to Ken Collins, Jack Layton, Frank Murray, Denny Sullivan and Mele Vojvodich for their participation in *Black Shield*. The posthumous award to Jack Weeks was accepted by his widow. The Legion of Merit was presented to Col Slip Slater and to his deputy, Col Amundson. In addition, the USAF's Outstanding Unit Award was presented to members of *Oxcart*'s 1129th Special Activities Squadron, also known as 'The Road Runners'.

The long-standing debate concerning whether *Oxcart* or a programme known as *Senior Crown* should carry forward the strategic reconnaissance baton had at last been resolved after three often bitter years of wrangling. The single-seat A-12 was vanquished.

The 'new kid on the block' was the two-seat SR-71A (the back seat being occupied by a Reconnaissance Systems Officer, or RSO). This aircraft boasted an enhanced reconnaissance gathering capability, featuring a nose-mounted high resolution ground mapping radar, in addition to cameras and ELINT gathering equipment. When combined, these systems gave the USAF a tri-sonic, simultaneous, synoptic reconnaissance-gathering platform.

In early March 1968, SR-71s began arriving at Kadena to take over the *Black Shield* commitment.

A-12 Article Number 129 (60-6932) successfully completed six of the 29 operational missions flown during *Black Shield*. The jet did not return to the United States from Kadena with its sister A-12s, however, as it disintegrated over the South Pacific a month after the last *Black Shield* mission had been flown. This particular photograph was the first one ever released (in 1982) of an A-12 (*Lockheed*)

Five SR-71s are seen on Lockheed's Burbank production line in 1965 (*Lockheed*)

EARLY DAYS IN OKINAWA

It is impossible to overemphasise just how vital to US national intelligence agencies *Senior Crown* (codename for the SR-71 programme) reconnaissance missions were during the Cold War. Implicit in this is also the highly sensitive nature of such sorties. It therefore almost goes without saying that all *Senior Crown* operational missions were highly regulated. Strategic Air Command (SAC) was both a major command of the USAF and a JCS-specified organisation. Headquarters USAF assigned SAC the responsibility for all strategic reconnaissance, and the command executed its mission under the supervision and guidance of the Chief of Staff, USAF.

In part, the Commander-in-Chief SAC (CINCSAC) was directed 'to prepare plans for strategic aerospace reconnaissance for which the Air Force is responsible (electronic, weather, visual, aerial, photographic, cartographic, reproduction and related activities) to meet the global requirements of the Department of Defense'.

As a specified command, SAC received assignments directly from the JCS, which included photographic and signal coverage of selected areas, together with global upper atmospheric sampling. Requirements for individual reconnaissance programmes were specified and outlined in operations and fragmentary orders, and through its Strategic

This historic photograph, taken on 27 May 1967, depicts the initial cadre of officers assigned to the 9th SRW. The pilots are standing in the middle row, with their paired RSOs immediately behind them. 9th SRW CO, Col Bill Hayes, is standing in the centre of the front row (*USAF*)

Reconnaissance Centre (SRC) at Offutt AFB, Nebraska. Headquarters SAC exercised operational control over all such missions, supervising their planning, scheduling and execution, unless such functions had been specially delegated in a SAC operational order.

Specific SR-71 operations were planned by specialists in the aircraft's branch at the SRC in response to tasking by the JCS, initially in support of the SAC Single Integrated Operational Plan (SIOP – the nuclear deterrent), the Defense Intelligence Agency (DIA), the Commander in Chief Pacific (CINCPAC), Seventh Air Force, Military Assistance Command Vietnam and US Air Forces in Korea (COMUSKOREA). Senior Officers at the SRC participated in twice-daily meetings at 0730 hrs and 1530 hrs to review current mission tasking, planning and weather. Once the SRC had completed the mission planning process, details were forwarded to the JCS for final approval.

The SAC units chosen to operate the SR-71 were the 1st and 99th Strategic Reconnaissance Squadrons (SRS) of the 9th Strategic Reconnaissance Wing (SRW) at Beale AFB, near Sacramento, California. The 99th SRS flew the aircraft from June 1966 through to March 1971, when it was deactivated and its assets transferred to the 1st SRS.

As with the earlier *Oxcart* programme, three aircraft would initially be deployed to Kadena, where a detachment designated Operating Location 8 (OL-8) was established. This followed the numerical designation pattern of SAC's overseas reconnaissance locations. During the 20 years of SR-71 operations from Okinawa, the detachment was re-designated OL-RK (RK standing for Ryukyus, which is the island chain that includes Okinawa) on 30 October 1970, and then OL-KA on 26 October 1971. Finally, it became Detachment 1 or 'Det 1' of the 9th SRW in August 1974 – a title that it retained until 1990, when the SR-71 fleet was retired.

The operational deployment of SR-71s to Okinawa also resulted in the aircraft being given its nickname 'Habu' after a dark poisonous pit viper indigenous to the Ryukyu island chain. Although the nickname 'Blackbird' has long been publicly associated with the SR-71, that title has been shunned by crewmembers and others closely connected with the *Senior Crown* programme, who favoured the serpentine monicker.

It was from this location that SR-71 operations in the Southeast Asia theatre would be conducted, and both crews and aircraft were rotated through the detachment, from Beale. As the two squadrons neared operational readiness, decisions were made by Col Bill Hayes (CO of the 9th SRW) and Col Hal Confer (Director of Operations) as to which crews would be the first to be deployed to Kadena. Eight crewmembers were selected, and they began training for the deployment by performing simulator sorties depicting the oceanic route they would fly.

It was decided that the crew who ferried the first jet to Kadena would also fly the first combat sortie over North Vietnam. The predetermined mission sequence would also include a fourth crew in the line-up that would travel to OL-8 in a KC-135 tanker. Each SR-71 departure would be backed-up by a 'spare' (the fourth crew) should the primary jet have to abort due to NO GO discrepancies such as inlet malfunctions.

Two days before *Glowing Heat* – a codename reserved for SR-71 positioning flights – six tankers were flown to Hickam AFB, in Hawaii. Air refuelling (AR) support for the SR-71 was provided by KC-135Qs,

Majs Buddy Brown and Dave Jensen deployed the first SR-71 to Kadena, safely delivering '978' to the Okinawan base on 9 March 1968. According to ground rules established back at Beale, they were also due to fly the first operational sortie over North Vietnam, but fate was to rob them of that honour (*USAF*)

KC-135Q tanker support was essential for most SR-71 missions. This is a typical pre-contact position taken up by the receiver before slowly moving forward to the contact position, at which point the tanker's boom operator would fly the boom into the open refuelling receptacle. Connection with the boom also established a secure intercom link between the tanker and the 'Habu'. A total of 56 KC-135Qs were procured by the USAF to support SR-71 operations (*Author*)

and SAC codenamed these tankers *Giant Bear*. Initially, three units were designated to perform this vital task – the 903rd Air Refueling Squadron (ARS) at Beale, the 306th ARS at McCoy and the 909th ARS at Kadena. On 1 July 1971, support was increased to four units – the 9th and 903rd ARSs at Beale, the 306th ARS at McCoy and the 70th ARS at Little Rock.

The four crews chosen to conduct the first deployment agreed to draw straws so as to leave the choice of who would go first in the hands of Fate. Maj Dave Dempster held the four straws of varying length and the RSOs from each of the other three crews drew one. With 'the luck of the draw', Maj Dave Jensen's straw decided that he and Maj Buddy Brown would fly the first jet across 'the pond', and they would also hopefully fly the first OL-8 sortie from Kadena. Maj Jerry O'Malley and Capt Ed Payne would fly the second SR-71 and Majs Bob Spencer and Ruel (Keith) Branham the third. Dempster was left with the short straw, so he and pilot Lt Col Jim Watkins would ride the tanker unless one of the crews had a 'sick' jet.

Command of OL-8 would be alternated between the 9th SRW's wing commander and vice commander (and later the Deputy Chief of Operations). The first detachment CO would be the wing's vice commander, Col Charles Minter, and Col Carl Estes would be the director of maintenance. With the tankers safely at Hickam AFB, Maj Harlon Hain (the 1st SRS operations officer) set up a down-range radio station on Wake Island, some 2000 miles southwest of Hawaii, to provide emergency radio coverage. All was now ready for Brown and Jensen to make their record-breaking five-hour flight across the Pacific, the sortie being flown at speeds twice as fast as the existing official world record.

DEPLOYMENT

At 1000 hrs on the day prior to their departure, Brown and Jensen (along with back-up crew Watkins and Dempster) received their pre-mission briefing. Since this was the 9th SRW's first operational deployment, the briefing was attended by the wing commander and many others. Mission planners briefed the entire flight profile for the sortie, which would begin at 1100 hrs on 8 March 1968. After take-off, the crew would head west from Beale to a point 50 miles north of San Francisco, where they would 'light the burners' for a dash to 75,000 ft to check that all systems were functioning normally, before descending to the first air refuelling.

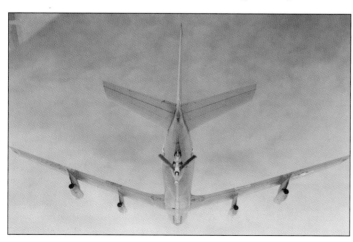

With a clean bill of health on the 'Habu', and a top-up of fuel from the tankers, Brown and Jensen would race to another refuelling northwest of the Hawaiian islands. They would then 'buddy cruise' with the tankers for an extra 30 minutes to take them to a point where they would be 'single-engine capable' to the island of Iwo Jima, which was their emergency divert base.

After the mid-Pacific refuelling, a third Mach 3 dash would take the crew to their third, and final, top up west of Wake Island, where a maximum off-load would give them enough fuel to reach either Kadena or an alternate base on Taiwan, should the weather have deteriorated over Okinawa. During the briefing, Brown and Jensen were told that the weather was expected to be good in the refuelling tracks, at Kadena and at their emergency landing bases, and that they could expect a comfortable crossing. After a maintenance briefing, the crews began 'official rest'.

At 0730 hrs on the 8th, the four crewmembers reported to the Physiological Support Division (PSD) for a final weather briefing and a maintenance report on their aircraft. This was followed by the standard preflight physical examination and high protein/low residue breakfast (steak and eggs and orange juice). After one last trip to the urinal, suit-up began. Two PSD suit technicians aided each crewmember as he donned his full pressure suit. A communications check and pressure suit integrity test confirmed that each garment was functioning properly, and after a ten-minute nap the crews were transported to their respective aircraft – Brown and Jensen to '978' and Watkins and Dempster to '980'.

After strapping in and connecting up, they began the normal challenge-and-response cockpit checklist that would take them through engine start, taxi and pre-take-off procedures. With engines revved to full military power and all instruments 'in the green', Brown released '978's' brakes and lit both afterburners. The SR-71 rapidly rolled down the Beale runway and lifted off into the vivid blue morning sky. Brown recalled;

'After crossing the California coast, I started our transonic acceleration climb profile to altitude. This portion of the flight was considered "mission critical" because the spikes, forward and aft inlet doors, inlet guide vanes and nozzles all had to check out prior to committing to the Pacific high-flight. Everything was "up tight", so we were on our way.

'Shortly after levelling off at FL750, we picked up the tanker's ARC-50 radio signals and started getting ranging information to the aircraft, which was about 400 miles away. We had a solid "lock-on", so we made the radio-silent rendezvous. We pulled up into the pre-contact position, were waved in, got a contact and started our max off-load to a pressure disconnect. We took on about 60,000 lbs of fuel, said our thanks and goodbyes over the boom interphone, then started on our way to AR No 2. The second leg was uneventful, although the AR contact point was changed slightly due to a line of thunderstorms in the AR track.

'We again accelerated on our next leg to the third, and final, refuelling. Approximately 20 minutes after level off at 79,000 ft, I encountered a problem that could have forced me to land at Johnson Island. My right spike, for no apparent reason, went full forward. This caused a very large yaw moment by creating lots of drag. I checked my cockpit over and found a popped circuit breaker, which, when reset, brought the spike back to its normal "bottomed" position for high Mach flight.

'The third decel, AR and climb were also normal, but when we were back at altitude, I encountered another potentially serious problem. My left generator went "offline", and I couldn't reset it. This was a NO GO situation, which meant I should land as soon as was practical. My decision was to continue on because we were now less than 1000 miles (about 30 minutes) from Okinawa. I used my coded call sign and contacted "Mamma", informing them that "I was lost, but still making good time". We landed at Kadena with the failed generator, but the first SR-71 had

29

Weary after their long tanker ride, Lt Col Jim Watkins and Maj Dave Dempster finally arrived on the wet island of Okinawa on the evening of 16 March 1968. Col Charles Minter (the first OL-8 commander) is seen here presenting both men with their 'Senior Taxi Wings' – Watkins and Dempster had taxied out to Beale's hammerhead three times in '980' as back-up to cover the launch of the three primary 'Habus' (*Dave Dempster*)

Later christened 'Ichi Ban' ('Number One'), aircraft '974' was the last of the original trio of SR-71s to be ferried to Kadena. It was also the last one of the three to fly an operational mission over North Vietnam. By the time it had finished its first deployment with OL-8, the jet had amassed a healthy tally of 'Habu' mission symbols aft of the RSO's cockpit (*Lockheed*)

arrived, and was soon ready to start reconnaissance missions in Southeast Asia, and wherever else the National Authorities might require.

'We left Beale at 1100 hrs and reached Kadena at 0905 hrs – two hours earlier than take-off time, but it was the next day, because we had crossed the international date line. We beat the sun by a good margin.'

Two days later, O'Malley and Payne delivered '976' to OL-8. They had departed Beale much earlier in the morning and landed at Kadena at 0330 hrs Japan time. Spencer and Branham flew '974' in on 13 March, and three days later the KC-135 carrying Watkins and Dempster arrived at Kadena.

It was late in the evening, and raining hard, when the tanker unloaded its weary passengers. As the last two SR-71 crewmembers (who had made the long Pacific trip 'the hard way') stepped from the tanker to what should have been a 'rapturous welcome' from the others, they were met by a junior NCO, who was there to drive them to their Visiting Officers' Quarters (VOQ) in a blue USAF maintenance van. The newcomers felt deflated as the NCO murmured a weak apology for the sparse turnout, dismissing it as 'high workload due to operational requirements'. As they opened the door to their VOQ room, they were greeted by the entire complement of crewmembers and senior staff, who cried out the raucous wartime welcome, 'Hello Assholes. What took you so long getting here?' OL-8 was now fully manned, and it was time for a 'little celebration'.

Col Charlie Minter was the chief architect of most of the operating procedures for OL-8's crews. Those rules proved so well structured that most of them remained unchanged throughout the entire 22-year life of the Kadena operation. The maintenance teams from the 9th SRW that manned OL-8 were considered to be the cream of USAF maintainers. Col Carl Estes' hand-picked 'Habu' technicians had done high-priority work on the three jets as they arrived, and they were all ready for operations by 0900 hrs on 15 March 1968, when the unit was declared 'fully OR' (Operationally Ready).

On 18 March, OL-8 was ordered to fly its first operational sortie. As previously agreed, Buddy Brown and Dave Jensen began preparing themselves for the mission. As a hedge against crew illness or aircraft system failures, every operational sortie was backed up by a spare aircraft and a suited-up aircrew who were equally prepared for take-off orders. The standby crew on this

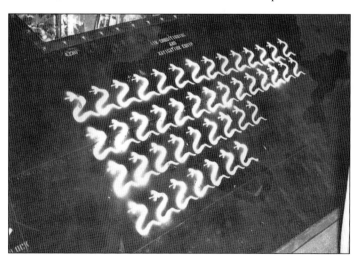

occasion was Jerry O'Malley and Ed Payne. Although everyone was 'all set' for the mission, it was cancelled by higher authorities and Brown and Jensen flew a 'Cathy' training sortie instead. As agreed at Beale, the next crew scheduled to fly was O'Malley and Payne.

TO WAR

On the morning of 21 March 1968, Maj Jerry O'Malley and Capt Ed Payne were driven out to the Little Creeks Hangar near the middle of the base. Precisely 50 minutes before take-off, the rear doors of the white PSD van opened and the two

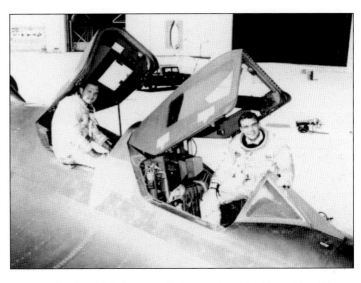

USAF fliers emerged wearing full- pressure suits, 'space' helmets and 'moon-boots'. The two crewmen walked into the old hangar, which was filled with all manner of high-tech support gear surrounding one of the world's most advanced operational military aircraft.

After shaking hands with Col Charles Minter, the four other SR-71 flight crewmembers present, key groundcrewmen and, finally, each other, O'Malley and Payne climbed the gantry ladder that took them up to the cockpits of SR-71A '976'. Carefully lowering themselves into their respective cockpits, the crew was assisted by white-coveralled PSD specialists, who swiftly connected them to their life-support gear, inter-communication leads and escape systems.

The exterior and interior preflight checks had already been completed by the 'buddy crew', who had 'cocked' the aircraft while the 'prime' crew was suiting-up. Half-an-hour before the scheduled take-off time, Jerry turned his attention to the pre-start checklist, reviewing certain important switch positions on his consoles and instrument panel. Those pre-start checks verified liquid oxygen and nitrogen quantities, as well as the positions of switches which controlled aircraft-specific systems such as the left and right aft bypass doors, the inlet centre-body spikes and forward bypass doors, suit-heat, face-heat and refrigeration for the cockpit and sensor bay environment control system. In addition, the moving-map projector was checked to ensure that it was loaded properly, the Stability Augmentation Systems (SAS) switched on and the TEB (Triethylborane) counters were each seen to display 16 units.

Although some of these checks were unique to the SR-71, many others were standard for conventional jet aircraft. Much of the challenge-and-response system of formal checklist reading was carried out for the purpose of putting 'on record' (via the cockpit voice recorder) that the many standardised procedural steps had indeed been performed.

While O'Malley was doing pilot tasks, Payne was at work in his 'office' performing HF and UHF radio checks, INS 'alignment' and aircraft Defensive Electronic Systems (DEF) checks. Other tests embraced checkouts of the TACAN radio-navigation system, camera exposure control systems, Astro-Inertial Navigation System (ANS) and the

Maj Jerry O'Malley and Capt Ed Payne successfully completed the SR-71's first operational mission when they overflew North Vietnam in aircraft '976' on Thursday, 21 March 1968 (USAF)

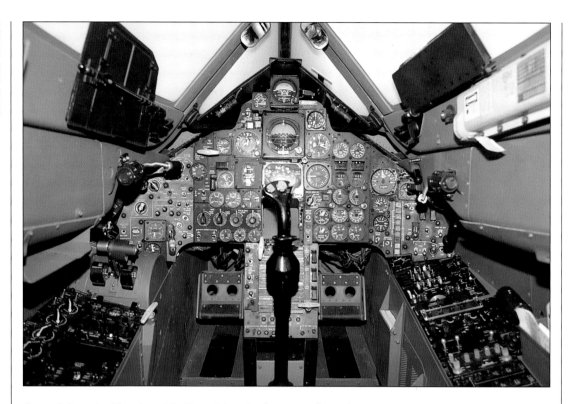

forward-down-looking view-sight. Payne's last checks were performed on the various reconnaissance sensors, canopy seal, Radar Correlator Display system, camera controls and, finally, the RSO's moving-map projector, which showed the entire pre-planned mission in considerable detail along a flight-sequenced photo-strip of a standard jet navigation chart.

During the aircrew's inter-cockpit checklist conversation, the crew chief was also plugged into the aircraft's interphone system (with head-set and microphone) through a phone jack-plug receptacle located in the nose-wheel bay. Through the use of this simple system, he was able to monitor their checks and responses prior to them commencing the engine start sequence. 'Interphone' – 'Checked'. 'Bailout Light' – 'Checked'. 'Triple Display System' – 'Checked'. 'Fuel Quantity' – 'Checked'. 'CG Limits' – 'Checked'.

As the clock ticked down to one minute before engine start, Payne called out the last four items. 'Oxygen Systems' – 'On and Checked'. 'Baylor Bar' – 'Latched and Locked'. 'Exterior Light Switches' – 'On'. 'Brake Switch Setting' – 'Checked'. The two J58 engines were ignited by revving each one up to 3000 rpm via two 400 hp Buick V8-powered start carts, which were spline-gear connected to a direct drive shaft in each engine's gearbox. The Buicks (working in series) sounded like racing cars when accelerated to high rpm during the J58's rapid 'spooling-up'.

At the designated moment, O'Malley said 'crank number two chief'. A Buick roared to life with an ear-splitting din in the confines of the Little Creek Hangar. Cocooned within the sound-proofed protection of his helmet, the pilot smiled as the rpm increased on the right engine, the steady climb levelling out as he eased the throttle forward into the 'IDLE' position on the quadrant. The fuel flow into the engine was timed to meet

The pilot's cockpit in the SR-71 reveals the aircraft's 1960s vintage, with little in the way of modern instrumentation. The A-12 cockpit was even more complex, as many of the sensor and navigation systems operated by the pilot were moved to the rear cockpit for the RSO to use in the SR-71 (*Author*)

with a 'thimbleful' of TEB, the successful use of which could be verified by a momentary flash of green flame from the exhaust nozzle of the starting engine, and by a visible 'down-click' on the right TEB counter (indicating one used shot of TEB) within the cockpit.

Less than ten seconds after the Buick had begun cranking, the engine was idling smoothly at 3975 rpm. Once the other engine was 'turning and burning', after-start checks were performed. 'EGT, Fuel Flow and Hydraulic System Pressures – All Checked. Flight Controls – Checked'.

As their cockpit canopies closed, minor problems appeared which threatened to jeopardise the mission. Firstly, Payne had no indication of cockpit pressurisation. That glitch was remedied by simply advancing the engine rpm, which duly inflated the canopy seals. As he searched through the GO-NO GO checklist to determine the importance of the other minor discrepancies, O'Malley said, 'Well Ed. Do you want to be the first guy to abort an operational sortie, or the first to fly one?' Payne's response was predictable. 'Kadena Tower, this is Beaver Five-Zero, radio check', to which the tower operator answered, 'Five-Zero you are loud and clear, and cleared to taxi'. He acknowledged with two unspoken clicks of his mic switch – a standard procedure used to minimise radio emissions on unguarded frequencies that could be monitored by Soviet 'fishing' trawlers that often lurked in international waters just off the coast.

Prior to the SR-71 moving out from the hangar, a ground technician released the scissor switch on the nosewheel knee and hand-guided the aircraft backward via a nosewheel tow-bar. Slowly, '976' was towed by a tractor (back end first) out of the hangar under the control of a tug operator clad in an aluminised fire-protective 'fear-naught' suit. As the groundcrew re-secured the nosewheel scissor switch, Payne called out the last checklist items. The crew chief disconnected his intercom link, removed the wheel chocks and signalled O'Malley that it was all clear to move out. The pilot eased '976' forward and checked the brakes in the first few feet of the roll out, after which he steered the jet down the taxi-way to the hammer-head run-up area adjacent to the end of the runway.

Payne got a 'starlight' from the ANS, indicating that the system had already searched and successfully 'acquired' three stars for triangular position referencing. His Present-Position-Indicator confirmed that everything was working fine, and that they were within 100 ft of track at

Majs Bob Spencer and Keith Branham touched down at Kadena in '974' on 13 March 1968, but it was not until 22 April that they managed to fly their first operational mission – also in '974' (*USAF*)

runway end. In the pre-launch engine run-up position, the wheels were tightly checked, the brakes held firmly and engine trim checks completed. Fuel sequencing, brake switches, pitot heat, battery and inverter switches were checked again. The INS's reference altitude was updated, and the crew sat ready to taxi forward to the number one position on the active runway for an 'on-the-second' take-off roll.

All eyes on, or around, Kadena were fixed upon the 'black jet'. A few minutes before take-off, the

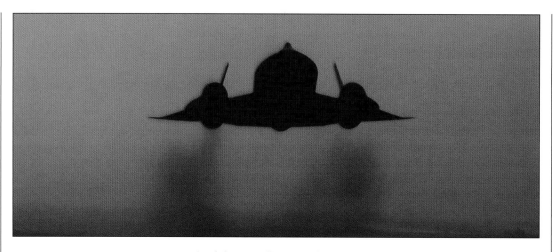

Another 'Habu' mission gets underway from Kadena in 1968 (*Lockheed*)

'mobile control' car was driven onto the runway by the spare crew, who then proceeded to conduct a runway-length 'foreign object' check for debris that might damage the tyres or engines during launch. The groundcrew then sledge-hammered the chocks free from the wheels and stowed them in the back of their ground-support 'bread van', before sending '976' on its way with a crisp salute. As the final countdown moved towards brake release, Kadena Tower called 'Five-Zero, you are cleared for take-off'. Payne answered 'Click-Click', and O'Malley, who had eased the throttles forward to 7200 rpm, released the brakes and said to his RSO, 'Military Power – Set. Tachometer, EGT, Nozzle Position and Oil Pressure – All Checked. We're on our way Ed'.

The pilot then moved the throttles forward to the mid-afterburner position, which resulted in a left-right yaw movement as each afterburner lit, accompanied by a tongue of flame glinting from the rear of each engine. 'Throttles to Max A/B', O'Malley said as the 'Habu's' take-off roll accelerated, followed by 'Decision Speed – Looks Good. No Problems', ten seconds later. As '976' approached 180 knots, O'Malley gently pulled back on the stick, whereupon the nose rose smoothly to ten degrees above the horizontal. At 235 knots he murmured 'Lift-off' and 'Wheels up', and retracted the undercarriage immediately to ensure that the 300-knot gear-door limit was not exceeded. In less than 25 seconds Kelly Johnson's 'masterpiece' was airborne on its first operational mission.

Once airborne, O'Malley reassured Payne that all systems were looking good, and that the engine instruments were checked. Immediately Kadena Tower called 'Beaver Five-Zero. Contact Kadena Radar'. Payne replied with two clicks on the mic, and selected Radar's frequency. 'Beaver Five-Zero, this is Kadena Radar. Squawk 2107'. He dialled the code on his IFF panel and pushed the 'Ident' button, whereupon the Kadena controller confirmed that the jet was cleared to proceed on track. He then chose a HF radio frequency for rendezvousing with the tankers.

At 0.5 Mach, O'Malley engaged the control surface limiters and saw the SURFACE LIMITER light on the tele-light panel extinguish. A crosscheck between he and Payne confirmed that both flight director platforms that powered their flight instruments were operational. O'Malley selected the Astro-Inertial Platform Gyro for instrument power and reference, while Payne used the secondary gyro platform for back-up.

Automatic fuel tank sequencing was checked and the altimeter set to 29.92 above 18,000 ft to ensure that all aircraft would have a standard reference for altitude separation. On their way to the refuelling area, O'Malley levelled '976' at FL 250 and maintained 0.90 Mach, taking up a heading toward the AR Control Point, where the KC-135s were orbiting. Payne, meanwhile, had activated his mission sensors.

For its first operational mission, the SR-71 carried a Goodyear Side-Looking Airborne Radar (SLAR) in the nose, a downward-looking, vertically-mounted Terrain Objective Camera in the centre fuselage ahead of the nose gear, and an AR 1700 radar recorder unit in the N-bay within the right chine. Behind the cockpits, in the P- and Q-bays, were the left and right 'Close-Look' Hycon HR-308B Technical Objective 'TEOC' cameras, touting a 48-inch (1219 mm) focal length lens. Finally, bays' S and T housed two Itek Corporation HR-9085 Operational Objective Cameras (OOCs). These high-resolution, three-dimensional panoramic cameras had a focal length of 13 inches (330 mm).

At this point in the mission, Payne was waiting for the reconnaissance systems and sensors to warm up so that he could verify their in-flight performance. It took six minutes for the radar to warm up, two minutes for the Recorder Correlator Display to function, two minutes for the Electromagnetic Recorder (EMR) to be ready and 20 seconds before the cameras could be tested. After six minutes, he pressed the Built-in Test (BIT) button for the radar, but it failed to work. Since it was not a primary sensor for this mission, the crew decided to proceed without it – they could rely on the ANS and Gyro Platform for navigation. Payne then checked the DEF system jammers.

First DEF A was turned on, and after warming up for two minutes, the S (standby) light illuminated. This was followed by the other defensive systems, DEF B, C, E and, finally, DEF G, which was powered up and declared operational. At that point Payne told O'Malley that the DEF System was ready – a definite 'GO' action on the GO-NO GO checklist.

A special covert radio-ranging system known as the ARC-50 had been specially developed to allow the SR-71 to rendezvous discreetly with KC-135Qs by giving azimuth and distance information to both crews as they approached one another in total radio-silence. Linking up southwest of Okinawa, the tanker started pumping the special JP 7 fuel into the SR-71's tanks immediately after the jet had safely connected with the boom. Having received 70,000 lbs of fuel, Payne recomputed the jet's centre of gravity (CG). The final part of the refuelling was conducted in near-tropical air mass, resulting in the SR-71 responding sluggishly to the military power settings on both engines as it cruised at 350 knots.

To overcome aerodynamic drag and the limited mil-power thrust, O'Malley engaged 'MIN-Burner' on one engine and cross-controlled slightly to overcome the off-set thrust – the added thrust made it easy to take on the last 10,000 lbs of fuel. At a prearranged time and position, and with 'Beaver Five-Zero' full of JP 7, the boom was disconnected. As the SR-71 dropped back and gently slipped clear of the tanker, the pilot lit both afterburners and pushed the throttles up to MAX, accelerating '976' to 0.90 Mach, before climbing to FL 330.

At 33,000 ft O'Malley eased the nose below the horizon into a 2500 ft per minute rate of descent to 'punch through the Mach'. The jet slid neatly through Mach 1 and the speed continued to build to 435 knots equivalent air speed (KEAS), at which point the pilot applied back-pressure on the stick. At 30,000 ft the descent was changed into a climb, and the Triple Display Indicator showed 450 KEAS, which was the standard speed for most of the climb to altitude. Having completed the so-called 'dipsy-doodle' manoeuvre, O'Malley re-engaged the autopilot and stabilised the climb angle to hold the 450 KEAS.

On reaching Mach 1.25, EGT and Compressor Inlet Temperatures (CIT) were noted. At Mach 1.7, inlet parameters and CG trim positions were monitored, followed by the manual setting of the aft bypass door controls and the locking out of the Inlet Guide Vane (IGV) switches. Finally, the DEF jammer systems were also rechecked.

At 60,000 ft, Payne switched off the IFF altitude read-out to ensure the security of the SR-71's altitude capabilities. Additionally, the aircraft's red-flashing anti-collision beacon was turned off and retracted to preclude heat damage to the lights, and to reduce the high-flying aircraft's visual signature. Reaching Mach 2.6 with the aft bypass door controls in the 'B' position, O'Malley established a KEAS bleed, which resulted in the air speed being decreased by ten knots for the gain of each tenth of a whole Mach number.

Their high altitude route took them east of Taiwan, north of the Philippines and out over the South China Sea. Skirting the east coast of China, and after passing Hainan Island, the auto-navigation function of the ANS and autopilot turned '976' smoothly right in a 35-degree bank onto a northbound heading, and the jet entered the Gulf of Tonkin. Continuing north, Payne peered through his view sight and located a large pier on the west side of Hainan that he had pre-planned as a visual-offset reference point to verify his track position. To his great satisfaction the pier was 'right on the money', the ANS flying the 'black line' within 50 ft of its centre. They had been travelling at Mach 3.0 up to that point at a height of 75,000 ft.

As they entered the Gulf, O'Malley started a cruise-climb to 78,000 ft and acceleration to Mach 3.17, preparing for a 'front door' entry into North Vietnam. Through his view-sight, Payne could see ship wakes on the waters below, and they could both hear the excited chatter of US combat pilots in heavy action way below them over Haiphong and Hanoi. With the tracking camera on for after-mission verification of their ground track, and with the ELINT and COMINT sensor-recorders already running, Payne switched the OOCs on ten miles prior to 'coasting in'.

Following a heading of 284 degrees, they crossed Haiphong at 78,000 ft, immune from any form of interception as they were travelling at the rate of a mile every two seconds. All the North Vietnamese

At least one Kadena-based SR-71 had a rearward-facing ciné camera mounted in the fuselage in an attempt to monitor SAMs being launched against it during overflights of North Vietnam. Note the fully aft inlet spike position at Mach 3, which was designed to maximise airflow capture in the rarefied conditions at 85,000 ft (*via Frank Murray*)

could do was watch on their radars. The DEF systems aboard '976' indicated that they were being tracked from the moment they crossed the coast by 'Fan-Song' radar units co-located with SA-2 'Guideline' Surface-to-Air Missile (SAM) batteries. Payne put out the correct ECM response and the radars failed to 'lock-on'. The weather below was perfect for a photo run, and as they flew over the harbour at Haiphong, Phu Kin airfield, Busundi airport and dozens of other targets in the vicinity of Hanoi, the exposure counters clicked down, indicating to Payne that the sensors were working 'as advertised' – it was going to be a perfect 'take'.

In just 12 minutes they had completed the first phase of the sortie as per the scheduled mission brief. Payne got ready to read the pre-descent checks to O'Malley as they exited North Vietnam. Crossing the Red River, O'Malley flicked the IGV switches to Lockout and Payne called out the checklist items. 'LN-2 quantity' – 'Checked'. 'Inlet Controls' – 'Auto and Closed'.

Jerry eased the throttles out of afterburner and set the EGT reading to 720 degrees Centigrade, the airspeed being allowed to decrease to 350 KEAS before starting the long gradual descent into Thailand. Carefully monitoring fuel tank pressure so as to avoid inflicting crush-damage on them as the jet descended into denser air, the crew reached 70,000 ft some 100 miles after commencing their descent. Now at Mach 2.5, O'Malley further retarded the throttles to 6000 rpm to hasten their descent.

The air-to-air TACAN's Distance Measuring Equipment (DME), as well as the ARC-50's DME ranging element, rapidly 'clicked' down the distance between '976' and the ever-dependable tankers, which were orbiting near Korat air base ready to 'pass gas' to their 'high and hot' receiver. Below Mach 1.7, O'Malley turned the forward fuel transfer, pitot heat and exterior anti-collision beacon light switches on. At 42,000 ft, and slowing through Mach 1.3, he checked the inlet controls and clicked the IGV switches to Normal after making a throttle adjustment. He then turned off the forward fuel transfer and prepared for refuelling.

Maj Craven Gibbons, flying the lead tanker, timed his turn to perfection just as '976' arrived at 25,000 ft a few miles behind and 1000 ft below the two KC-135Qs. Sitting slightly to the right, and a few hundred feet below in the pre-refuelling observation position, O'Malley noted the boom was extended and the 'Boomer' was nodding it up and down to indicate that he was ready for a radio-silent contact. He slipped smoothly in behind the trailing boom and stabilised in the pre-contact position, before moving forward.

Once 'plugged in', a secure interphone link-up was established between the KC-135 and the SR-71, and while much-needed fuel was being pumped into the thirsty receiver at the rate of 6000 lbs per minute, hearty words of congratulations were offered to the 'Habu' crew. O'Malley took 40,000 lbs of fuel from the first tanker and topped off from the second – a third aircraft was standing by to act as an emergency 'spare' should either of the primary tankers be unable to offload their fuel.

After each refuelling, O'Malley thanked the tanker crews. At the prescribed time and location, '976' left the KC-135s and headed out for another run to the north. The pilot repeated the climb and acceleration routine up to the prescribed altitude, on track for the second and final 'take' for the mission. This 'run' was to be flown over the DMZ between

North and South Vietnam, with a primary objective being to find the truck park that supported the transportation of supplies and troops down the north-south Ho Chi Minh Trail, and fed shells to the heavy guns that had been pounding the hell out of Khe Sanh.

For this run, the primary sensor was to have been the Side-Looking Radar (SLAR), which could penetrate the heavy jungle canopy. However, since the system had failed its BIT-test, its serviceability was questionable. Payne concluded, however, that no damage could be done to the system if he positioned it manually and took some shots on the off chance that it would find something. Soon after, the jet exited the 'sensitive' area and the crew made their way back to Okinawa.

Feeling justifiably proud of how well their mission had gone up to that point, O'Malley started his deceleration and descent towards Kadena with the expectation of a 'proper' first-flight mission success party at the BOQ. On contact with Kadena Approach Control, they were dismayed to find that the base was completely 'fogged in'. The pilot talked to the tower controller and then to Col Charlie Minter, who agreed to allow them to attempt a low visibility approach for a visual landing.

Using Ground Controlled Approach (GCA) radar assistance, O'Malley descended as low as was prudent into the fog, which the crews on the ground later reported was below the tops of the tanker tails only 30 ft above the ramp. Although the approach was good, O'Malley never saw the runway, and pushed the throttles forward to go back 'upstairs' to contemplate further options. Low on fuel, he called for the standby tanker that had been launched earlier just in case the weather at Kadena turned nasty. After link-up, he took on 25,000 lbs of fuel, while Payne copied a two-figure encoded number that told them the location of their divert airfield – Ku Kuan, on the island of Taiwan.

Two additional KC-135s were launched to accompany '976' to Nationalist China, the SR-71 adopting a tanker call sign as the number 'two' aircraft in a three-ship formation. This deception was undertaken to hide the inter-island diversion from SIGINT monitors on the Chinese mainland. As they made their way 'low and slow' with the tankers, the destination airfield's non-directional beacon returned the unexpected Morse Code identity signal of CCK. The tanker crew soon resolved this problem, however. It turned out that Ku Kuan had recently been re-named Ching Chuan Kang!

O'Malley asked the CCK tower for permission to land, and made a straight-in visual approach at 175 knots, before performing a smooth touch-down. After clearing the runway and lining up behind the lead tanker, he sandwiched '976' between two KC-135s as they taxied in. This unusual sight caused considerable confusion in the tower, particularly when one controller asked for the call-sign of 'the little black aircraft between the two tankers, which had replied with a tanker call sign'. While Payne was talking to the tower people, O'Malley dialled up the radio frequency of the SAC Command Post that had recently opened on CCK. He asked for the aircraft to be 'hangared' (for security reasons).

Since CCK was a PACAF (US Pacific Air Force Command) joint-tenancy base with the Chinese Nationalists, most of its hangars were already filled with C-130 Hercules transports. To clear a secure spot for the SR-71, a C-130 up on jacks had to be rapidly lowered back onto its undercarriage and rolled out of a hangar. This took 30 minutes to perform, which left the SR-71 standing in full public view close to the base perimeter fence with its engines still running. A crowd of at least 500 Taiwanese gathered 15-deep along a 300-yard section of the fence, all of whom were fascinated to see such a futuristic jet standing on their airfield almost within touching distance.

Once '976' was safely hangared, and a security cordon thrown up around the area, the first order of business was to download the 'take' and get it to the various processing facilities so that the 'goods' could be fielded out to the intelligence community as quickly as possible. The next priority was to get the jet and its crew back to Kadena. To accomplish that, a recovery crew flew in from Okinawa in a KC-135 the next day.

By then, the raw intelligence data had been despatched to Yokota AFB in Japan for processing by the 67th Reconnaissance Technical Squadron (RTS) – this until processed all SR-71 data until 29 March 1971, when the 548th RTG at Hickam AFB assumed this responsibility. The SLAR imagery was sent to Beale AFB for processing by the 9th RTS, before being sent on to Washington, DC for analysis by national-level agencies.

Meanwhile, back in Taiwan, O'Malley and Payne endured a night in CCK quarters that the latter described as 'remedial at best'. Having no proper evening clothes other than 'moon suits', they borrowed ill-fitting flight 'grow bags' and went to dinner wearing their white 'moon boots'. Things took a turn for the better the following day, however, with the arrival of their ever-resourceful Ops officer, Lt Col 'Beep-Beep' Harlon Hain, and his recovery team. He brought with him a full set of 'civvies' for both men, and got them booked into a first-rate hotel near the base. After two nights at CCK, '976' was ready for its ferry flight back to Kadena. The unrefuelled 'hop' was uneventful, but the reception by their friends and colleagues back at the Little Creek Hangar was 'superb'.

The post-mission intelligence results were also quite stunning. The SLAR that Payne had manually programmed had indeed worked. Its 'take' revealed the location of the heavy artillery emplacements around Khe Sanh, and a huge truck park which was used in support of those guns – both sites had eluded US sensors on other reconnaissance aircraft up to that point in time. Within the next few days air strikes were mounted against both targets, reducing their effectiveness dramatically.

After a 77-day siege, Khe Sanh was at last relieved on 7 April 1968 (two weeks after '976's 'discovery' sortie). As a result of their significant contribution to this highly successful mission, Maj Jerome F O'Malley and Capt Edward D Payne were each awarded the Distinguished Flying Cross. On its very first operational sortie, the aircraft had proven its value. It would continue to do so on a near-daily basis for the next two decades.

Soon after SR-71 missions commenced at Kadena, a tradition was born whereby a crew flew their first operational sortie with a necktie under their pressure suits. Upon their return, this was ceremoniously cut by CMSgt Bill Gornik, wheeling a mini Samurai sword. Here, Phil Loignon joins the club after his pilot, Don Walbrecht, had undertaken the experience moments earlier. This photograph was taken on 25 May 1968, the crew having flown their 'Habu' mission in '978' (USAF)

THE WAR CONTINUES

Following the success of the first 'Habu' sortie on 21 March 1968, fate was to intervene and frustrate the other OL-8 crews, who were desperate to fly their own operational missions. Indeed, almost three weeks passed before the next overflight of North Vietnam was undertaken by the SR-71, with all four crews being scheduled to fly operational missions in that time, only to have them cancelled and replaced with training sorties instead.

On 10 April 1968, Majs Buddy Brown and Dave Jensen were once again set as 'primary crew'. Maj Jerry O'Malley and Capt Ed Payne were suited up as back-up. Brown cranked '974's' engines precisely on time and taxied out of the 'Little Creek' area to run-up near the end of the runway. O'Malley and Payne were sitting in '976' waiting to hear that the primary crew was 'off and running'. Instead, crew chief TSgt Bill Campbell told them that '974' was taxiing back to the hangar.

While O'Malley and Payne were getting ready to roll, Brown and Jensen parked '974' nearby, the stricken jet being duly 'swarmed' over by most of the OL-8 maintenance force. Even Col Estes clambered on top of the jet with his ANS specialists and 'was working like a GI mechanic' to help replace the astro-inertial navigation set. Meanwhile '976' was ready.

'We got out there and were running a fast checklist when I happened to look up and here comes Buddy taxiing like a bat out of hell. It must have been a world record ANS change, but I was certain that Dave hadn't had time to get a "star light" because the system hadn't had time to go through

To facilitate ground handling, SR-71s were housed both at Beale and their permanent detachment locations in 'taxi-in, taxi-out barns'. Commencing another mission 'up North', this anonymous aircraft taxies out of the OL-8 barn at Kadena. The weather conditions seen here were not unusual for Okinawa (*USAF*)

all of its BIT checks yet', recalled Capt Payne. 'Charlie Minter, who was in the mobile control car, was obviously thinking the same thing. Since it was his duty as OL-8 Commander to put the best aircraft over the target, he leapt from the car and wrote "YOU GO" on an 8 x 10-inch pad, which he held up to Jerry and I, and "YOU STAY" on the other side, which he showed to Buddy and Dave.'

Climbing away, O'Malley and Payne elected to adopt the primary aircraft's call sign, since they had made that jet's take-off slot. They reasoned that the tankers would be expecting that call sign, and that they would minimise confusion by keeping '974's' identity. Unfortunately, the call sign change did not help Bill Boltersiders in the Command Post, who had to despatch a coded report to HQ SAC immediately after take-off. In his uncertainty as to which jet had actually departed, he had to wait for Col Minter's return from the flightline before having the necessary details to set HQ SAC straight. O'Malley and Payne were again on their way to North Vietnam on the SR-71's second combat sortie.

They coasted-in near Saigon, made a shallow turn to the right to fly northbound across the DMZ towards Vinh and then on to Hanoi. There was no shortage of high priority targets, including Phuken and Ying-By airfields and a steel works near Hanoi. Unknown to the crew, President Johnson had stated that day in a broadcast that no US strike aircraft would fly further north than the 19th parallel. His decision had caused confusion within military circles as to the meaning of 'strike aircraft'.

The 'ground pounders' at higher headquarters decided to play it safe, and sent out an HF radio message intended to stop all US aircraft from overflying enemy territory. Payne received a coded message from *Sky King* on the *Giant Talk* network, but he was too busy flying at 33 miles a minute over the primary target area to decode the message, which instructed them to abort the mission. Moments later, the autopilot initiated a programmed turn steering them southward. With a few moments between high-workload events, Payne told O'Malley about the abort order. After completing the turn, they exited North Vietnam near Dien Bien Phu and headed for their tankers over Thailand.

The two fliers' spirits had been high throughout the sortie, particularly since their good luck had enabled them to fly both operational OL-8 missions performed to date. The sortie had been 'a piece of cake' so far, or so they thought until O'Malley eased back the throttles to the pre-assigned descent RPM. At that moment both engines rumbled slightly in a compression stall and immediately flamed-out.

An air-start required 450 KEAS and 7 PSI on the compressor face to get things 'turning and burning' again. That meant getting down to denser air, where those higher aerodynamic values could be achieved. O'Malley pushed

As insurance against a ground abort compromising the completion of a vital operational 'Habu' mission, a ground spare frequently accompanied the primary aircraft out to the hammerhead at Kadena during the Vietnam War (*USAF*)

the nose down hard and Payne recalled seeing the artificial horizon instrument showing 'all blacks'. As they rode the aircraft down to lower altitudes they decided that if O'Malley could not get an air-start, Payne would call 'MAYDAY' at 23,000 ft, and they would 'punch out' at 14,000 ft. At 40,000 ft, the pilot gave the throttles a nudge, which in turn gave the engines positive fuel flow and a shot of TEB for ignition. There was no response. O'Malley tried again as they were passing through 30,000 ft, but still nothing.

'By now we were both getting anxious', Payne explained. 'I saw the altimeter go through 26,000 ft and I was getting set to say "MAYDAY! MAYDAY! MAYDAY!" I got the word "MAY" out when I felt the jet shake a little. Realising that Jerry had finally got something going, I didn't finish the rest of the message. A glance at the altimeter showed us just below 23,000 ft, and still descending rapidly. Just then Jerry said "I've got one of them started." Shortly afterwards he got the second engine fired up, and when we hit 20,000 ft we had both engines running fine.'

Having received the 'MAY' of Payne's message, the tanker crews knew that all was not well with the 'Habu'. This realisation was confirmed as they monitored the air-to-air TACAN's DME ranging. Ordinarily, the SR-71 would make a 'hot' rate of supersonic closure on the tankers, slowing notably only in the final 30 miles. The DME meter would normally be clicking over at between 20 to 30 miles per minute during the early part of the deceleration. Instead, it quickly slowed to a closure rate of eight miles per minute. That speed meant the 'Habu' was 'low and slow' well before it should have been, way up in 'bad guy' territory.

Payne remembered, 'We got our act cleaned up, and the first transmission we received from the tankers was, "Are you guys okay?" I answered, "No". They asked "What can we do?" I answered, "Turn north". The double-engine flame-out and rapid descent had left "976" down at a 'gas-gobbling' 20,000 ft over northern Laos, some 300 miles short of our planned AR contact point. We climbed back to 26,000 ft and headed south. I recall that the lead tanker navigator was a woman. I'm sure they must have violated operating procedures coming that far north without some form of fighter cover, but we were damn glad to see them.

'By the time we reached the tanker, "976" had less than 8000 lbs of fuel left in its tanks. The KC-135Q turned in front of us and the boomer plugged into our AR receptacle in a "heartbeat". We drained 80,000 lbs of JP 7 out of two tankers, and even used a little from the spare – perhaps a record off-load. We used the extra gas because we had to lengthen the air refuelling track from Laos to mid-Thailand. Had we just filled up and climbed for home, we wouldn't have been able to fly the profile properly, so we just stayed behind those beautiful tankers until we reached the originally planned disengagement point.'

While O'Malley and Payne were refuelling, they discussed what might have caused the double-engine flame-out, and what would be the preferred action to get home safely. The RSO was in favour of staying with the third KC-135Q and flying all the way back at 0.90 Mach to meet some Kadena-launched spare tankers. The pilot, on the other hand, believed that they should fly a normal profile to help determine the cause of the problem. O'Malley discussed at length what data he wanted Payne to record, and just prior to the final decel back into Kadena he began reading out RPM, EGT and fuel flow information. He eased back the throttles and the engines spooled down normally. They landed without further incident, thus ending the SR-71's second operational sortie.

That double flame-out foreshadowed a spate of similar problems that would follow over Laos, and would earn the 'Habu' the nickname of 'Lead Sled' back at the SAC Reconnaissance Center.

With the first two operational missions under their belts, O'Malley and Payne were relegated to flying test hops for the duration of their tour to ensure that the other crews had an opportunity of accumulating some combat time. The following week, Buddy Brown and Dave Jensen were scheduled to fly a 'double looper' over North Vietnam.

Getting airborne in '978' at 1100 hrs on 18 April, all went well until it was time to decelerate for their first Thailand refuelling. The tanker notified them that the AR contact point had been moved due to thunderstorms in the AR area. As they began to decelerate, the left generator went off-line and could not be reset. This failure was followed by a double-engine flame-out. Jensen transmitted the necessary codes stating that they were going to make a precautionary landing at Takhli air base, since generator failure was a 'land as soon as practicable' abort item.

Without power they lost cabin pressurisation and their 'moon suits' inflated, which made movement in the cockpit awkward. As they descended toward an altitude where the engines could be restarted, Brown requested that the tankers come north to give them additional fuel after their early and rapid descent. At 35,000 ft he was able to restart the engines. He then adjusted the aircraft's centre of gravity for subsonic flight, and called Takhli Approach Control, informing them of their impending arrival. The tower controller told them that the tankers had already alerted the base Command Post, and that they were ready to receive them. On approach, the nose gear's down-lock light failed to illuminate, so Brown made a low pass by the tower to have the gear visually checked 'down', before making an uneventful landing.

Since the CIA had a 'secure compound' on the airfield from where it conducted U-2 operations, Brown was able to use one of their hangars. A recovery team soon arrived from Kadena and readied the SR-71 for its flight home. As they were preparing to depart, the head of the Agency's detachment told Brown, 'If you don't tell anyone you were here, I won't either'. He laughed at the 'typical cloak and dagger' remark, and thanked him for the first-rate support on their interrupted 'Habu' mission.

Twenty-four hours later, following cancellations and disappointments, Jim Watkins and Dave Dempster finally got airborne in '974'. They topped-off their tanks near Kadena and headed for North Vietnam. Arcing around Hainan Island on their right, they entered the Gulf of Tonkin and reversed left onto their penetration track. This 'front door' entry took them over Haiphong and Hanoi, exiting via Dien Bien Phu.

Like earlier flights, everything went well until it was time to come down for aerial refuelling. As soon as Watkins slid the throttles out of afterburner, there was an enormous bang, followed by another double-engine flame-out. He got both engines started up again after wiping 50,000 ft of altitude off the altimeter's reading. The tanker crews responded immediately to the emergency call, heading north without fighter escort back into the 'bad lands' of northern Laos.

Whilst the 'Habu' was on the boom taking on three tons of fuel a minute, Watkins had time to reflect on the incident, which could have ended in disaster. At that point he said to his RSO, 'Davey, I think I might know what happened, and if I hold a couple-hundred more RPMs above what it says in the check-list the next time I come out of 'burner, I might be able to keep the engines alive, and we can complete the mission. What to you think?' Dave replied, 'Let's give it a try and do the next run.'

It seems that Jim Watkins had the first glimmer of an idea that would later be proven when Don Walbrecht and Phil Loignon flew Vietnam-to-Thailand descents without a problem in late May.

On 27 April, Bobby Brown and Dave Jensen flew their second operational sortie, this time in '976'. As they started their descent into Thailand, they again experienced another double-engine flame-out and another failed generator. Forced to land at Takhli for the second time in nine days, Brown insisted that he had not come to join the CIA, but to enjoy their hospitality! On leaving the base two days later, he saluted them with a 'max burner' climb out that 'left them all smiling', as the low-fuelled 'Habu' climbed steeply away from its new-found second home.

MISSILES

At just after 0900 hrs on 26 July 1968, Majs Pat Halloran and Mort Jarvis launched in '974' for what was to be their first operational sortie. However, during the course of conducting a BIT check on their DEF suite, the RSO detected a systems failure. As mentioned earlier, this was a NO GO item on the check list, so he continued to recycle the equipment repeatedly in the hope that the problem would clear, but to no avail.

With time running out, the crew finally had to admit defeat, and literally just five minutes short of their mandatory time to call for the spare to launch, they aborted. Consequently, at 1008 hrs Majs Tony Bevacqua and Jerry Crew launched in '976' to replace '974' on the planned 'double-looper' over North Vietnam. On their first pass, Crew warned Bevacqua that a SAM fire-control radar had locked onto them. Almost immediately he said, 'We've been fired upon'. The defensive systems performed as advertised, but the pilot was unable to see the SA-2, which ended up well behind them.

During refuelling Crew asked Bevacqua if he intended to complete the sortie, since their next

On 26 July 1968, whilst participating on an operational mission in '976' over North Vietnam, Majs Tony Bevacqua and Jerry Crew became the first SR-71 crewmembers to be positively targeted by an SA-2 SAM, as captured in this photograph taken by their Terrain Objective Camera (TROC) (*USAF*)

track would again take them back over the position from which they were fired upon. The pilot replied, 'Why Not? They missed us.' On the next pass there was no reaction from any SAM battery. Back on the ground at Kadena, Bevacqua recalled;

'As we got out of the aircraft, we knew that the commander was aware of the incident. The first thing he asked was, "Did you see anything?" We said we hadn't, but we knew that it was for real. We were later told that the nearest of the two missiles was about one mile away.'

This was the first occasion that an SR-71 had definitely been fired upon, and, by chance, the terrain-tracking camera took a picture of the SA-2s, recording Bevacqua's 'first' for the record books. Halloran and Jarvis launched again in '974' two days later, and completed their first operational sortie – a 5.3-hr flight – flawlessly.

By the autumn of 1968, airframes '974', '976' and '978' had each amassed close to 300 flying hours with OL-8. In so doing, they had easily validated the concept of long-range, triple-sonic, high-altitude strategic reconnaissance within hostile airspace. Their sensor systems had acquired intelligence data of national significance that had directly influenced the conduct of many air and ground operations.

The dedicated professionalism of the maintenance teams working for Col Estes, and the high quality systems maintenance conducted by specialist company technical representatives, kept the deployed SR-71s in top condition, but there was certain 'heavy' depot-level maintenance tasks that lay beyond the capability of OL-8. For deep maintenance tech-order modification work to be carried out, the three jets had to return to Lockheed's Palmdale Plant 42. A complex every other day swap-out exercise codenamed *Glowing Heat* was effected in late September, with '974', '976' and '978' being replaced by '962', '970' and '980'. These aircraft were similarly replaced in April 1969 by '971', '975' and '979'.

The escalation of the Vietnam War generated an increase in the demand for timely, high-quality reconnaissance imagery. OL-8's SR-71 establishment was therefore increased in the spring of 1970 from three to four aircraft ('969', '972', '973' and '974'). The next three years would prove in many ways to be the detachment's 'Golden Era'.

Returning to 1968, on 20 September Majs Dale Shelton and Larry Boggess completed their first operational sortie in SR-71 '980'. However, 30 minutes into their second operational flight on 4 October they were just approaching the KC-135Q to top off after take-off when a coded message came through on HF radio from *Sky King* (SAC's *Giant Talk* network) telling them to abort their mission and return to Kadena. The RSO checked the authenticity of the message, but could not re-transmit on HF since Shelton had already started refuelling. Boggess recalled;

'When we didn't answer immediately, we got a curt UHF radio call from the Kadena Command Post asking us if we'd received an earlier HF message transmission. We disconnected from the boom, dumped some fuel and returned "970" to Kadena.'

It seems that intelligence sources had discovered that the enemy knew of the 'Habu's' intended route, which would take the jet directly over an active SAM site. Although SR-71s had been fired upon on an earlier sortie, it was deemed that the North Vietnamese had too much of an advantage on this occasion.

Some of the crews who were fired upon by SA-2s spoke of seeing the SAMs through the RSO's view sight and the pilot's rear-view periscope. The missiles had to be fired 30 miles ahead of the jet so at reach the SR-71's altitude by the time it arrived overhead the SAM site. Two white trails would appear well ahead of the 'Habu', but they were normally not seen by the pilot since the aircraft's nose blocked his ground view ahead.

As the missile approached, the RSO could see it rising by looking through his down-and-forward-looking view sight. When the SAM detonated (usually above and behind), the pilot got a quick glimpse of the explosion, which would appear to billow out and then implode on itself. This visual effect came about because of the rate of speed at which the jet passed the point of detonation. It was strange to see, but crews reported that it was also comforting to know that the SAMs were ineffective because of the very long firing lead the missile-shooters needed to boost the SA-2 to altitude to 'point-intercept' the 3000-ft-per-second target.

AIRCRAFT LOSS

Throughout the early 1970s, OL-8's Vietnam sortie rate averaged two flights per week. The nature of high-speed flight ensured that those combat sorties would never become 'routine to the point of indifference'. OL-8 lost its first 'Habu' after more that two years of Kadena operations, which included 200+ operational and training sorties.

On 10 May 1970, Majs Willie Lawson and Gil Martinez had completed one pass over North Vietnam and then refuelled '969' near Korat air base. The pilot had initiated an afterburner climb to prepare for a transonic 'dipsy-doodle'. Thunderstorms had by then rapidly built up across Thailand, and no matter where they looked, a solid bank of cloud enshrouded the heavy thunder cells, which towered up to 50,000 ft.

Even an SR-71 needed climb distance to get above the clouds, and the dip-manoeuvre gave the aircraft a head-start on achieving the airspeed and Mach needed for a higher rate of climb. The 0.90 Mach preliminary climb was sluggish with a full fuel load, and Lawson eased '969' into a slightly steeper climb to zoom up over a notch in a 30,000 ft-saddleback of connecting clouds between vertical storms in order to stay clear of the cells ahead. At that moment, the jet entered turbulent clouds and both engines flamed out.

In heavy turbulence, without engine thrust, the aircraft's angle-of-attack increased. Suddenly, the nose rose into a dreaded pitch-up, from which there was no recovery. Both crewmembers ejected safely and landed in the vicinity of U-Tapao air base. Resplendent in their silver

Having been deployed from Beale to Kadena by Majs Jim Shelton and Tom Schmittou on 24 September 1969, aircraft '969' was the first of three SR-71s to crash – on 10 May 1970 – whilst flying from Okinawa. The jet was performing its 11th 'Habu' mission at the time of its demise (USAF)

'moon suits', they recruited the aid of a Thai local who was driving a Saamlor (a three-wheeled vehicle common to Thailand) and hitched a lift back to U-Tapao. They were then flown back to Kadena in a KC-135. Upon their arrival, Col Hal Confer (the OL-8 commander) and the entire unit had gathered to welcome them back. The pitch-up problem would ultimately cost the USAF four aircraft in 26 years of SR-71 operations.

KINGPIN

Son Tay prison camp was located 23 miles west of Hanoi, and it had gained notoriety for housing dozens of US PoWs. It was the subject of numerous SR-71 'takes' as intelligence analysts endeavoured over two years to establish just how many prisoners were being held in the stockade. On 10 June 1970, a feasibility study group was convened by the Special Assistant for Counterinsurgency and Special Activities (SACSA), to look into the possibility of 'springing' the Son Tay inmates.

A further planning group was set up in early August to review reconnaissance imagery provided by Teledyne-Ryan's *Buffalo Hunter* reconnaissance drones and SR-71s. The low-flying drones were used sparingly over the target area for fear of alerting the North Vietnamese to the possibility of a future raid. The SR-71, with its long-axis camera capability, was an ideal vehicle for obtaining spot photos of the camp.

In the last ten days leading up to the raid on 21 November 1970, intense reconnaissance efforts were conducted, but every attempt was thwarted by poor weather. Continuous cloud cover had concealed Son Tay's targets from the 'Habu's' high-altitude cameras, and two low altitude drones never returned. Nevertheless, a mission was mounted, employing Florida-trained US Special Forces troops who used five HH-53 Jolly Green Giant helicopters in an attempt to rescue the 65 inmates thought to be at Son Tay. Unfortunately, the camp was empty.

It was first thought that there may have been an intelligence leak at Hurlburt AFB, Florida, where a mock prison had been constructed for rehearsing the raid's swift action. However, it later transpired that the camp had been empty for some time due to the threat of flooding from a

Pre-strike SR-71 imagery of the Son Tay prison compound (*USAF*)

47

nearby river. The lack of timely photo-intelligence was a great embarrassment to Brig Gen LeRoy Manor's Son Tay 'raiders'.

MORE IMPORTANT SORTIES

Flying time in the SR-71 (especially combat flying) was always considered a premium commodity among the 20 crews in the 9th SRW, and they would 'wheel-and-deal' with the staff schedulers for additional sorties. Although Southeast Asian sorties accounted for the majority of the OL's flight hours, that area was not the exclusive domain of the 'Habu'. Majs Bob Spencer and Butch Sheffield were particularly pleased to be selected for one such prize sortie on the night of 27 September 1971.

After completing the ritual post-take-off air refuelling in '980', they climbed away from the tankers on a northerly track opposite to the standard route down south into Vietnam. US intelligence had obtained details of the largest ever Soviet naval exercise to be held in the Sea of Japan, near Vladivostok. Undoubtedly, such an event could provide a rich source of intelligence data, and an SR-71 was the ideal vehicle with which to stir the Soviet fleet's defensive systems into action.

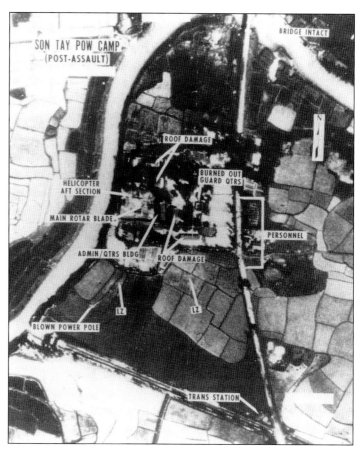

Post-strike SR-71 imagery of Son Tay following the unsuccessful raid on 21 November 1970 (USAF)

National security officials were especially interested in obtaining fresh data on the signal characteristics of the new Soviet SA-5 SAM system, codenamed 'Gammon'. If technical details pertaining to the signal characteristics of its radar's frequency, modulation, pulse-repetition frequency (PRF), pulse-repetition interval (PRI) and other factors could be measured, it might be possible to develop an effective ECM device to reduce or negate the SA-5's highly-touted capabilities. The main problem was that the various ELINT recorders carried on the SR-71 filtered the vast range of electromagnetic emissions transmitted from all sources and actuated special recorders only when receiving certain signal types.

To solve this problem, Maj Jack Clemence (an inventive Electronic Warfare Officer) who worked in the 9th SRW's Electronic Data Processing (EDP) Center, jury-rigged one of the ELINT sensors by electronically cutting and splicing the pulse receiver's filtering system, which allowed it to receive a continuous-wave signal.

The possibility of night disorientation (caused by inlet unstarts and other hazards) over the dark northern Pacific led mission planners to restrict most turns to a 25-degree bank limit while night flying at Mach 3.2. The two crewmembers of '980' concentrated their attention on the naval target area off Vladivostok while slicing through the night in full afterburner. If they maintained their current inbound track toward the Soviet port and turned at a 25-degree bank, they would overfly the USSR, crossing high over the Khrebet Sikhote Alin and exiting the area into the Sea of Japan, before returning to Kadena. As they bore down on the target area, dozens of Soviet radars were switched on to record what appeared to be a certain violation of sovereign Soviet airspace.

The deception worked well, with '980' turning as planned, and thus failing to violate Siberian airspace due to the jet being programmed to roll into a full 35-degree bank, instead of the previously recorded 25-degree banks, so as to remain in international airspace.

On his approach to the target area, Spencer noted to his great dismay that the oil pressure in the right engine was dropping. Nevertheless, he pressed on. When the crew completed their target run, and were heading south toward home plate, he rechecked the critical oil pressure gauge. By then its reading had fallen to 'zero', which was bad news indeed. After a brief consultation with Sheffield, he shut the engine down.

Having already stirred up a hornet's nest of defensive activity with their feinting pass over the Soviet's Pacific Fleet, the crew was now forced to descend and continue the rest of the flight at subsonic speeds, where they would be 'sitting ducks' for any fast jets that might be scrambled to intercept the oil-starved 'Habu'. To make matters worse, they encountered extreme headwinds that rapidly depleted their fuel supply. Sheffield calculated that a recovery back to Kadena was completely out of the question. Instead, they would have to divert into South Korea.

The OL-RK commander had been monitoring '980's' suddenly-slowed progress, and as the 'Habu' neared Korea, US listening posts reported the launch of several MiGs from Pyongyang, in North Korea, in what appeared to be an intercept attempt. USAF F-102 Delta Daggers were immediately launched from a base near Hon Chew, in South Korea, and vectored into a position that put them between the MiGs and the SR-71. It was later established that the MiG launch had been unconnected with the 'Habu's' descent.

Spencer recovered '980' into Taegu, in South Korea, where the base commander had already received a call concerning his special visitor, and was therefore ready to receive the SR-71 and its crew. Their EMR 'take' turned out to be

Whilst flying '980' on the night of 27 September 1971, Majs Butch Sheffield (left) and Bob Spencer really stirred up a hornets nest in their quest to acquire the signal characteristics of the then new Soviet SA-5 'Gammon' SAM (USAF)

'monumental'. In all, Spencer and Sheffield had 'sniffed-out' emissions from 290 different radars. Of even greater significance to Western intelligence analysts were the 'beautiful' SA-5 signals that they had successfully captured – the first ever detected.

IN-THEATRE PROCESSING

On 5 April 1972, Lt Col Ed Payne (by then, OL-8's chief of intelligence) received a phone call from a friend at Norton AFB, in California, who spoke in indirect references about 'some blue boxes that would soon make Ed's job easier'. The call was so obscure that he did not know what his Norton contact was trying to tell him until a week later when he received a top secret message.

President Nixon had just signed the Defense Appropriation Bill, within which provision had been made for OL-KA to be equipped with a Mobile Processing Center that could perform post-mission processing at Okinawa, rather than having to send the material to Japan or the US.

The computer portion of Mobile Processing Center 1 (MPC 1), housed in eight vans, had been despatched from Beale to Kadena in time for the arrival of the first three SR-71s deployed to the island back in March 1968. Contained within these was the CDC-3200 computer equipment needed for SR-71 mission planning, sensor programming and providing an initial scan of the SR-71's ELINT collection.

The remaining 15-van portion that was to now be sent to OL-KA contained additional equipment necessary for processing the SR-71's High Resolution Radar (HRR) and photo-reconnaissance collections, and for preparing a detailed analysis of the ELINT collection. These were airlifted in by two Military Airlift Command (MAC) C-5 Galaxies. The Adage Graphics Terminal AGT-30 was flown in from Travis AFB aboard a MAC C-141 Starlifter.

Just prior to the arrival of Payne's 'Blue Boxes', an area of Kadena was rapidly prepared for the MPC's many vans. The blue trailers were quickly unloaded and placed in position, where they were interconnected to function as an in-theatre 'recce-tech' unit. At 1845 hrs on 18 April, Payne was on the phone to NPIC informing them that he was ready for quick response intelligence processing. The OL could now process ELINT, COMINT and black-and-white imagery.

With the MPC 'up and running', imagery was fast processed as soon as the 'Habu' landed, being 'wet-read' by the photo interpreters, who supplied an Initial Photo Interpretation Report (IPIR) on the highest priority targets. Before the MPC was deployed, SAC would fly the SR-71 film to the 548th RTG at Hickam AFB for processing and a preliminary readout – a process that took, on average, 40 hours. With the MPC in operation, this was cut to 11 hours.

This intelligence would be communicated in plain English on a secure telephone to 'appropriately cleared' persons on Secretary of State Henry Kissinger's staff, who could if necessary provide a report to the President within four hours of an SR-71 overflying key targets. Such direct reporting of 'hot' intelligence was a remarkable achievement for the time.

Duplicate sets of photo negatives were immediately produced, with a set then being flown to Eielson AFB, in Alaska, where it was transferred to another courier aircraft and flown to Washington, DC to be sped onward to the NPIC. Another courier would deliver a set of negatives to the 12th RTS at Saigon for the next day's air strike planning. Other high-priority recipients were Fleet Intelligence, Pacific (FINCPAC), the 532nd RTS at Udorn air base, the 544th RTS at Offutt AFB, in Nebraska, SAC's B-52 force in Southeast Asia, the CIA, the JCS, the President and the National Security Council.

The MPC also accomplished an initial ELINT scan for high-threat signals within three hours of the SR-71's return to Kadena. The complete Mission Intercept Report Electrical (MIRE) was produced within 20-24 hrs, but final follow-on technical ELINT reporting was still conducted by the 9th RTS at Beale.

BOOMING THE 'HILTON'

During the late spring of 1972, a number of intriguing and highly-classified sorties were flown from Kadena to North Vietnam on 2, 4 and 9 May. Each mission involved two primary aircraft and an airborne spare. Their objective was to 'lay down' two sonic booms within 15 seconds of one another as a signal to key prisoners of the notorious 'Hanoi Hilton' PoW camp.

During the 4 May mission, Majs Tom Pugh and Ronnie Rice approached the target area in aircraft '978' at 75,000 ft from the south, while Majs Bob Spencer and Butch Sheffield, maintaining 80,000 ft in '980', flew across the target from the southeast. Meanwhile, Lt Col Darrel Cobb and Maj Reggie Blackwell were the airborne spare in '978'. They were to cross the 'Hilton' at 70,000 ft from the west should either of the primary aircraft have to abort.

The mission and the timing of the two booms were so critical that Cobb and Blackwell flew all the way to the target area. A pre-arranged codeword had been established which would indicate that their services would not be needed. When that word was transmitted, Cobb broke off his run short of the target area.

Majs Ronnie Rice (left) and Tom Pugh had a very close-call on 15 May 1972 when they were forced to over-fly Hanoi at just 41,000 ft (12,497 m) following a double engine flame-out in '978' (*USAF*)

All three missions were deemed to have been 'entirely successful', accomplishing their objective within the very tight time constraints – reconnaissance gathering was deemed to be of secondary importance to the creation of the boom on these sorties. Some 36 years after the event, it is still unclear as to why these missions were flown, or what the double booms were meant to signify to the PoWs.

On 15 May 1972, Majs Tom Pugh and Ronnie Rice were airborne in '978' on the former's 236th SR-71 sortie. They were flying a routine 'Giant Scale' mission, which was scheduled to be a 'double looper' up through the Gulf of Tonkin for a 'front door entry' into North Vietnam. As the aircraft approached Haiphong, Pugh's concern over a strange cyclical hum in the interphone system was relieved when the generator bus-tie circuit split, allowing independent operation of each of the 60 KVA AC generators, one of which had been responsible for the varying frequency – hence the hum. Freed of the AC bus load sharing, the system seemingly returned to normal. The GO-NO GO checklist allowed the mission to proceed.

While Tom was maintaining Mach 3.18 at 79,500 ft, a generator failed. That failure was a mandatory abort item, however, so the crew began making provisions for a divert into Thailand. Just over a minute later the other generator failed, and now they were in real trouble. Emergency AC and DC power did not come on-line, and the fuel boost pumps stopped the flow of JP 7 to the engines. Without electrical power the SAS cut out, and lacking boost pump pressure, the fuel-flow to both engines stopped. They quickly flamed out. To add to their grief, the inlet spikes went full forward and, as '978' began pitching and rolling rapidly, Pugh knew the aircraft was approaching the limits of its supersonic flight envelope. He instructed Rice to 'get ready to bale . . .', but the intercom system failed before he could finish the statement.

Pugh gently held the control column while struggling to fly the jet (without causing further pilot-induced oscillations), and while also try-ing to reach the all-important 'Standby-Electrical Switch' located on his right-hand panel. To reach that critical switch he had to move his left hand off the throttles and onto the control column in order to free his right hand so that he could restore some electrical power to the aeroplane. This accomplished, he initiated a gentle 'needle ball and airspeed' turn towards a 'friendly piece of concrete'. Having descended to 41,000 ft, and slowed to just Mach 1.1, Pugh managed to get one generator back on-line and both engines re-lit. He then reaccelerated '978' to Mach 1.7 to exit the area as quickly as possible. Pugh crossed Laos to recover '978' into Udorn air base without further problems.

The serious nature of the malfunction necessitated that they return to Kadena subsonically. As they set off with two KC-135Qs (one carrying the recovery team), the crew heard another SR-71 diverting into U-Tapao air base.

'978' is seen at Udorn air base, in Thailand, following its diversion on 15 May 1972 (*USAF*)

SR-71 '978' was dubbed 'Rapid Rabbit' because of the Playboy bunny emblems chalked onto its twin tails (*Lockheed*)

The tanker carrying the maintenance team peeled away from '978' and headed back to Thailand to recover the other jet. At their post-flight analysis, Pugh and Rice learned that they had overflown Hanoi at 41,000 ft. They had been extremely lucky considering the number of SAMs encircling the city. It appeared that the North Vietnamese radar operators and their Soviet advisers had been 'asleep at the switch' during '978's' mid-altitude pass over of the world's best defended city. The aircraft had pulled off a lucky escape from what appeared to be an easy shoot down situation. Pugh and Rice were each awarded Air Medals for Meritorious Achievement in 'the successful landing of their disabled aircraft'.

On 30 May, '978' was at the centre of yet another scary episode. Majs Bob Powell and Gary Coleman were approaching Hanoi for a 'front door' entry when the SAS failed. They had just entered a 30-degree bank at Mach 3.2 and 81,000 ft when the aircraft started porpoising. As Powell struggled to master the destabilised flight characteristics, he had to decelerate and descend to where the aircraft would be more manageable. Coleman radioed the tanker with a delayed rendezvous time because they would be approaching at subsonic speeds. Powell completed a somewhat ragged aerial refuelling and trailed a spare tanker to the east coast of Vietnam, where they filled the tanks and slogged their way back to Kadena at 0.9 Mach (logging six-and-a-half flying hours).

On 20 July 1972, '978's' luck finally ran-out. While returning from an operational mission, Majs Denny Bush and Jimmy Fagg were informed of excessive cross-wind landing conditions as they approached Kadena. On touch-down, Bush activated the aeroplane's large braking parachute in a rapid deploy jettison technique to prevent '978' from weather-cocking sharply into the wind and running off the side of the runway.

Unhappy with the first touchdown, he jettisoned the parachute, pushed up the power and 'took it around' for another landing approach. Although he successfully touched down on the second attempt, the crosswind was so strong that he was unable to keep the wind-cocked aircraft on the runway. During this 'off-runway' landing roll-out, one set of main wheels struck a low concrete structure, severely damaging the landing gear and causing substantial damage to the aeroplane itself. Both crewmembers clambered out unscathed, but '978' was written-off.

Less than two months after its diversion into Thailand, '978' was written-off in a landing incident during high crosswinds at Kadena on 20 July 1972 (*Lockheed*)

The 'salvageable' wreckage was subsequently flown back to Norton AFB via Yokota air base on 3 November in C-5A Galaxy 69-0007, and parts were later used rather ignobly as spares for other 9th SRW SR-71s. The remaining sections of the airframe were scrapped in Okinawa.

LINEBACKER AND BEYOND

The 'flexible response' strategy adopted in the early 1960s by the Kennedy Administration to the escalating conflict in Vietnam caused SAC to examine the tactical potential of its strategic bombers in that war. By mounting two multiple-ejector racks under the wings of certain Stratofortresses (in place of missile pylons), a further 24 bombs could supplement the 27 bombs that could already be hauled internally, thus nearly doubling the B-52F's bomb load.

As the situation in South Vietnam worsened and Operation *Rolling Thunder* commenced, the JCS decided to deploy the modified B-52Fs to Andersen AFB, Guam, in February 1965. Codenamed *Arc Light*, the aircraft could be used to strike targets in North Vietnam in reprisal for terrorist action against US personnel in the south.

An ineffectual bombing raid was also mounted by a large number of fighter-bombers against Viet Cong base camps near Black Virgin Mountain on 15 April 1965. Soon after, commander of Military Assistance Command, Vietnam, Gen William Westmoreland obtained permission from Secretary of Defense Robert McNamara to use B-52s in support of tactical operations in South Vietnam.

The first big strike took place on 18 June 1965 when 30 Boeing bombers flew a 12-hour/5500-mile round trip from Guam to the Ben Cat Special Zone in Binh Duong Province, northeast of Saigon.

As the *Arc Light* sorties increased in frequency, a modification programme known as *Big Belly* got underway back in the US. Between December 1965 and September 1967, 82 B-52Ds received new radar transponders for ground-directed bombing, as well as bomb-rack modifications. The latter increased their carrying capacity from 15 bombs weighing 27,000 lbs to a 108 bombs weighing 60,000 lbs.

On 1 April 1966, the 28th and 454th Bombardment Wings deployed to Guam and began flying regular *Arc Light* sorties. In addition to the great increase in firepower that these *Big Belly* bombers represented, the sortie rate also grew from 450 to 600 flights per month. Seven ground radar-directed bombing sites called *Combat Skyspot* were established, the first one coming on line at Bien Hoa in March 1966. These sites, working in conjunction with the B-52s' new radar transponders, helped to improve bombing accuracy.

On 11 and 27 April 1966, B-52s struck North Vietnam for the first time, hitting targets in the Mu Gia Pass – the keystone of the notorious Ho Chi Minh Trail supply network. The B-52 sortie rate increased as the ground war continued to deteriorate, and by February 1967 more than 800 flights were being flown per month. Meanwhile, Guam had reached its saturation point in regards to the number of B-52s that it could

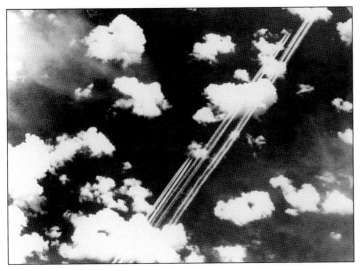

A cell of three B-52s in standard combat formation is captured on film by an SR-71's Terrain Objective Camera as they cross into North Vietnam some 50,000 ft (15,240 m) below the 'Habu' during a *Linebacker I* mission (*USAF*)

support. Thereafter, additional jets were deployed to U-Tapao air base at Sattahip, Thailand. A year later McNamara approved yet another increase to 1200 and then finally 1800 B-52 sorties per month.

On 1 November 1968, President Johnson called a halt to *Rolling Thunder* operations against North Vietnam. Target emphasis for the B-52s now changed to *Commando Hunt* operations, which were flown in an effort to stem the tide of men, equipment and fuel being infiltrated into South Vietnam via a supply network in Laos.

Eight months after the election of President Nixon in November 1968, Secretary of Defense Melvin Laird cut the B-52 sortie rate to 1400 per month. Two years later, it was reduced to 1000 sorties, and many jets and crews returned to the US.

In early 1972, however, an enemy build-up along the Laotian trail network indicated an imminent offensive. Gen Westmoreland's replacement Gen Creighton Abrams and Adm John McCain (CINCPAC) requested additional *Arc Light* sorties to forestall this rising threat. On 8 February the JCS authorised 1200 monthly sorties, and ordered 29 more B-52s to Guam. In a major invasion effort on 30 March 1972, the enemy hit South Vietnamese positions in Quang To, Kontum Pleiku and Binh Long provinces, prompting President Nixon to order a resumption of the bombing of North Vietnam – a policy that had been in abeyance since 1 November 1968.

As the situation worsened on all three fronts, B-52Gs were deployed for the first time. This increase brought the bomber force to 133 aircraft, which could fly as many as 2250 sorties per month.

In an operation codenamed *Linebacker I*, five B-52 strikes were launched – the first on 9 April against petroleum storage facilities and the railway marshalling yard at Vinh. This was followed by a raid codenamed *Freedom Dawn* on 12 April that hit Bai Thuong airfield. Four days later, *Freedom Porch Bravo* targeted petroleum, oil and lubricant facilities around Haiphong. Then, on 21 April, *Freighter Captain* launched strikes against the Hamn Rong transshipment point and the Thanh warehouse area. Two days later, *Frequent Winner*, revisited the targets hit on the 21st. *Linebacker I* was the first time that B-52s had ventured into the heavily defended Hanoi-Haiphong area.

SAC was requested to increase the number of SR-71 sorties to obtain imagery for bomb damage assessment during the new offensive. On 8 May, as the war escalated, President Nixon ordered that routes into and out of North Vietnamese harbours should be mined. The next day, in an operation codenamed *Pocket Money*, the JCS directed that drones and the SR-71 should photograph, on a daily basis, the ports of Haiphong, Hon Gai, Gam Pha, Dong Hoi, Quang Khe, Vinh and Thanh Hoa to identify the shipping channels in readiness for US Navy mining operations.

One week into the operation, the JCS designated the SR-71's High Resolution Radar (HRR) as an acceptable sensor for this purpose. This was the first occasion that the JCS had specifically directed that the HRR should cover a predetermined intelligence target, and by so doing, they signalled that the technology had officially come of age.

In June, the JCS required the SR-71 to photograph communication and logistics supply lines between North Vietnamese ports and Chinese border areas. Throughout this time, the SR-71 also used its sophisticated electromagnetic reconnaissance (EMR) system to collect ELINT as part of SAC's *Combat Apple* SIGINT collection operation in Southeast Asia that also utilised U-2 and RC-135 platforms.

As the situation on the ground deteriorated, additional B-52s were deployed to the region, and by late June 200 of the giant eight-engined bombers were in-theatre chalking up 3100 sorties per month. They were also having a decisive effect on the north's invasion.

On 21 April 1972, Air Force Logistics Command (AFLC), in conjunction with the SR-71's Advanced Systems Program Office, began flight-testing a prototype Capability Reconnaissance Radar (CAPRE). Manufactured by Loral, the new unit promised a significant increase in resolution over the earlier Goodyear GA-531 installation, then operational with the SR-71 fleet. The 12 evaluation flights conducted within the United States with the radar prototype (jet '975') were successfully completed by AFLC on 15 July 1972, and on 11 August, Majs Bob Powell and (RSO) Gary Coleman flew '975' to Kadena as part of the autumn *Glowing Heat* aircraft rotation. Onboard was the new radar, deployed for the first time to undertake its operational evaluation.

The first of these sorties was launched at 1545 hrs the very next day, the crew consisting of Majs Bob Cunningham and (RSO) George 'GT' Morgan. By November, the new system had demonstrated capabilities that far exceeded those of the earlier PIP radar, and accordingly, HQ SAC directed that the prototype CAPRE unit should be retained by the detachment until production sets became available for operational use.

In total, five other CAPRE units had been contracted by SAC, and plans called for the final unit to be delivered by May 1973. However, the production radars experienced a 23 per cent failure rate during AFLC certification – most of the problems were attributed to the failure of a heat resistant epoxy that caused the radar's antennas to malfunction. Before the production units could be deployed to Kadena, SAC insisted that ten successful flights from Beale must first be accomplished. As a result, the first CAPRE production model was not delivered to the 9th SRW until 5 June 1973, thus missing the June *Glowing Heat* aircraft rotation.

In late October 1972, President Nixon called a halt to the bombing north of the 20th parallel in anticipation of a truce. As a hedge against the talks becoming deadlocked or breaking up, he also ordered the JCS to plan new strikes against the North that would concentrate on the Hanoi-Haiphong areas. On 13 December 1972, the North Vietnamese Delegation walked out of the Paris Peace Talks (throughout the long period of negotiations, North Vietnam had used the time to rebuild and strengthen their badly damaged military infrastructure). Two days later, Nixon ordered the execution of *Linebacker II*. Initially planned as a three-day maximum night effort for B-52s, this operation actually lasted a full

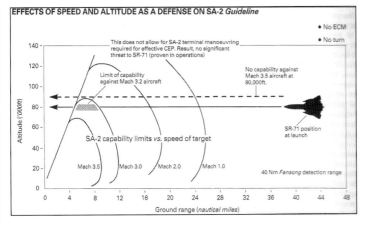

EFFECTS OF SPEED AND ALTITUDE AS A DEFENSE ON SA-2 *Guideline*

This graph clearly outlines some of the difficulties endured by North Vietnamese SA-2 crews intent on trying to 'bag' a 'Habu'. As this diagram shows, a SAM battery had no chance of hitting an SR-71 when the aircraft was flying at 90,000 ft, and only a limited chance of success when the jet was at 80,000 ft thanks to its Mach 3+ top speed (*Lockheed*)

During the final phase of *Linebacker II*, B-52 formations adopted so-called compression tactics. On the night of 26/27 December 1972, 120 bombers hit nine separate targets in the Hanoi area in ten waves from seven different directions in just 15 minutes. This awesome concentration of firepower, coupled with extremely effective ECM coverage, resulted in not a single B-52 being shot down (*USAF*)

11 days. Its primary aim was to cut off the supply of arms and ammunition at their source, thus strangling North Vietnam's war effort.

On Day One (18 December), 121 B-52 sorties were flown. Two chaff corridors were sown by F-4s, but 100-knot winds blew the protective curtain away before the bombers arrived. B-52G 'Charcoal 1', leading nine other Guam-based aircraft against the Yen Vien/Ai Mo warehouse area, was hit by two SA-2s, and thus became the first Stratofortress lost to hostile action in the war. Two other bombers were also shot down by some of the 200 SAMs launched that night.

On Day Two of the campaign, 93 B-52s hit targets that included the Radio Hanoi broadcasting station, as well as Kinh No, Yen Vien, Bac Giang and Thai Nguyen. Another 200 SA-2s were fired, but no aircraft were lost. However, on the night of 20 December six B-52s fell to SAMs. By Christmas Eve (Day Seven of the campaign) 11 B-52s had been shot down. After a 36-hour pause over Christmas, operations resumed. Using revised tactics, 113 aircraft battered ten different targets in seven 15-minute waves. Two more B-52s were lost to SA-2s despite the fact that they had been supported by more than 100 fighter-bombers, which were used to suppress SAM batteries in the Haiphong area.

An hour before midnight on 27 December 1972, *Giant Scale* mission GS663 got underway when SR-71 '975' lifted-off Kadena's runway on what would prove to be the only 'Habu' night sortie of the entire Vietnam War. Col Darrell Cobb and RSO Capt Reggie Blackwell's mission objective was to conduct a coordinated EMR/HRR sortie to determine if the North Vietnamese had acquired new equipment or employed updated procedures for the SA-2s that were responsible for destroying so many B-52. To achieve this, their arrival over the Haiphong/Hanoi areas was timed at precisely the same moment that 60 B-52s were to begin dropping their bombs on the railway marshalling yards at Lang Dang, Duc Noi and Trung Quant, as well as the Van Dien supply centre and three nearby missile sites.

With North Vietnam's defensive radar systems running at full stretch to cope with the raid, intelligence planners reasoned that this would be an ideal time for such a sortie. In addition, the SR-71's unmatched ECM suite could provide additional electronic support for the B-52s.

As they arrived over the collection area on schedule, Cobb and Black-

well observed numerous SA-2 firings. During the fleeting moments when they were passing over the immediate target area, the crew was able to radiate a blinding ECM blanket using their advanced defensive systems. During the course of the raid, only one Guam-based B-52 was lost. Cobb and Blackwell landed back at Kadena at 0239 hrs. Later that day they learned that their mission had produced a wealth of intelligence data, which included the discovery of two unique target emitters that had been instrumental in the downing of the B-52s.

The two sixty-bomber raids launched on the final two nights of *Linebacker II* saw all B-52s return safely to their bases. Following the action on the night of 29/30 December, the North Vietnamese government expressed a willingness to return to the negotiating table. The B-52s had flown 729 sorties during the 11 days of *Linebacker II* (340 from U-Tapao and 389 from Guam). Thirty-four separate target areas had been hit by the Stratofortresses, which had dropped 13,395 tons of bombs. The North Vietnamese had fired hundreds of SA-2s, destroying 15 bombers (nine B-52Ds and six B-52Gs) and damaging nine others.

The stunning onslaught unleashed by the USAF during *Linebacker II* drove the North Vietnamese negotiators back to the Paris Peace Talks, where they again engaged in deceptive negotiations whilst their compatroits attempted to recover from the 'war-ending' destruction of their supply lines and munition storage areas. A record of *Linebacker's* enormous level of destruction was faithfully recorded by the 'Habus'. The B-52s had won the war at that point, but their victory was given away at the Paris Peace Conference. The conflict in Vietnam ended for the United States when the Paris Agreement was signed on 27 January 1973, which committed the withdrawal of US forces from South Vietnam.

The agreement included the release of US prisoners of war within 60 days, the formation of a Four-Party Joint Military Mission, the establishment of an International Commission of Control and Supervision, the clearance of mines from North Vietnamese waters and free elections for all Vietnamese. For the SR-71, it brought about a reduction in target tasking, followed by a reduction in the number of Kadena-based aircraft from four to three. Another jet returned home soon after, leaving two SR-71s to perform stand-off reconnaissance.

Following the ceasefire, Det 1 continued to gather bomb damage assessment imagery of B-52 strikes in Cambodia, in addition to monitoring the status of various North Vietnamese-occupied airfields. These included Tchepone, in Laos, together with Cam Lu and Kham Doc in South Vietnam. The Plaines De Jarres in Laos also received regular visits from the SR-71 in order to monitor the infiltration of men and material moving from North to South Vietnam.

This certificate accompanied the award of an Air Medal to RSO Maj Reggie Blackwell following his successfully completion of the only SR-71 night mission of the entire Vietnam War on 27 December 1972 (*Reggie Blackwell*)

On 17 February 1973, Majs Bud Gunther and Tom Allocca departed Kadena at 1300 hrs on mission GS696 – a four-hour operational sortie in aircraft '975'. Of particular interest on this mission was the area around Khe Sanh airfield. Again, the intelligence community was extremely pleased by the 'take' once it had been processed, as it revealed that adjacent to the airfield, AAA emplacements had been built. A new unnumbered supply route and truck park were also discovered, together with a probable cave storage area and two operational SA-2 sites – the first to be discovered in this area since the late spring of 1972.

Such a high-level of activity documented by '975's' cameras led the analysts to conclude that the communists intended to make Khe Sanh a permanent control point for operations in the south of the country.

The terms of the ceasefire prohibited US reconnaissance aircraft from overflying North Vietnam, so the SRC devised a route for the SR-71 that involved six 45-degree bank angle turns that allowed the jet's camera and SLAR systems to obtain imagery from well inside the country during peripheral missions.

To ensure that North Vietnam was adhering to the terms of the Paris accords, the JCS directed that two SR-71 sorties were to be conducted in April 1973. The first of these – GS722 – was flown by Majs Buck Adams and Bill Machorek in aircraft '971' on the 19th. However, due to heavy cloud cover, intelligence obtained during this sortie was almost entirely generated by the prototype CAPRE high-resolution radar. It proved that the Viet Tri rail and road bridge, located 30 miles northwest of Hanoi, had been interdicted since Majs Bob Cunningham and Jimmy Fagg had photographed it in '975' during their 23 January mission.

Imagery collected during the latter sortie had also caught 11 MiG-21s parked on the western alert apron at Phuc Yen airfield. However, analysis of the HRR imagery obtained on the 19 April sortie suggested that no aircraft were then on alert. Photo interpreters noted that a similar situation had prevailed at Phuc Yen during *Linebacker II*, when the MiGs had been removed from the base's apron areas and hidden in cave storage facilities. However, after the bombing halt and the signing of the peace accords, the MiGs were once again parked on the alert aprons. Intelligence specialists therefore concluded that the absence of fighters at Phuc Yen on the 19 April was consistent with an increase in their alerted air defence posture.

Clearing skies enabled a conventional camera configuration to be carried on the second monitoring sortie. This would enable analysts to crosscheck the HRR imagery obtained five days earlier. Consequently, *Giant Scale* flight GS725 got underway on 24 April 1973, when Majs Pat Bledsoe and (RSO) Reggie Blackwell left Kadena at 1145 hrs in aircraft '963'. Additional targets covered by this five-

'963' is seen on short finals as it comes in to land at Kadena on a typically humid day. Note that a vertical flow pattern has been generated in moist air at the root of the outboard wing section. The pilot has also set a small amount of rudder deflection. This aircraft participated in a number of *Giant Scale* flights during *Linebacker II* and immediately post-war, serving with OL-KA between 21 August 1972 and 13 June 1973 (*USAF*)

hour thirty-minute flight were the Ben Thuy transshipment point, the petroleum products storage facilities at Vinh and Bai Thuong airfield.

Yet again the SR-71 proved its worth at Bai Thuong airfield, located 77 miles southwest of Hanoi, when '963's' cameras photographed large quantities of military equipment and vehicles. The target imagery also revealed that bomb craters on the main runway and parallel taxiway had been repaired. Three coastal petroleum barges were noted in the vicinity of the Vinh bunkering pier, and a moderate amount of activity was also recorded at the Ben Thuy transshipment point, four miles east of Vinh.

Aside from the *Giant Scale* missions already detailed in this chapter, within two weeks of the ceasefire, Pacific Command's ELINT Center had requested that SAC provide increased electronic reconnaissance of various signal threats emanating from Laos. On 9 February 1973, SAC instructed the SRC to schedule two SR-71 ELINT missions per week against Laotian objectives for the remainder of the year.

SS *MAYAGUEZ* INCIDENT

On Monday, 12 May 1975, the US-registered freighter SS *Mayaguez* was stopped by Khmer Rouge gunboats as it steamed in international waters some 60 nautical miles southwest of Cambodia, near the island of Poulo Wai in the Gulf of Siam. The merchant ship was boarded, and the next day, under the control of its captors, the *Mayaguez* was moved to a point about two miles off the northeastern tip of Kaoh Tang Island.

The ship was initially located by two F-111s diverted from a routine training mission the day after the vessel's seizure. Thereafter, a round-the-clock surveillance plan was put into operation to monitor the *Mayaguez's* movements. Just before dawn on 15 May an assault was launched on two beaches at the northern tip of Kaoh Tang and a search was made of the vessel in a bid to release the ship's crew. However, a small Thai fishing boat had been used to move the crew to the Cambodian mainland the day before, and the Marine boarding party found the freighter to be empty.

As the assault force conducted a heliborne assault on Koah Tang, it encountered stiffer resistance than had been anticipated from a much larger and well-fortified group of Khmer troops. In an action lasting 14 hours, 15 US troops were killed, three listed as Missing In Action (MIA) and 50 wounded. Four H-53 helicopters were also downed. Whilst fighting raged on the island, offshore, the Thai fishing boat returned the ship's crew unharmed to the frigate USS *Harold E Holt* in a gesture which seems to have been unconnected with the battle for their release.

The importance of this assault resulted in an SR-71 mission being scheduled to monitor the strike on Koah Tang. It was flown on 19 May by Capts Al Cirino and (RSO) Bruce Liebman in '961', and their mission was to photograph the after effects of the raid. Their 'take' was to prove extremely useful during debriefings.

Despite the war in Southeast Asia having ended in August 1973, SR-71s from OL-KA continued to conduct occasional overflights of Cambodia. Although never officially admitted, the large numbers

Deployed to Kadena twice, '963' was assigned to OL-KA in 1972-73 and from 13 August 1974 through to 16 July 1976. Seen here taxiing out at the start of yet another 'Habu' mission in 1975, the aircraft is presently displayed at Beale AFB as a memorial to the 9th SRW (*Steve Myatt*)

of American troops listed as MIA continued to be a source of concern for the US government. This reason, together with occasional 'sightings' of MIAs and rumours of isolated prison compounds in inaccessible jungle areas, proved strong enough for various US intelligence agencies to request that such flights be sanctioned.

One such mission was flown by Majs B C Thomas and (RSO) Jay Reid in '976'. The 5-hour 48-minute flight was conducted on 24 November 1980 – some seven years after the cessation of hostilities. Unfortunately for the relatives of those left clinging to such hope, no substantive evidence was produced by the jet's sensors to back up such speculation.

OTHER MISSIONS

In May 1978, Vietnam began a series of border skirmishes with Kampuchea, and in late December these escalated into a full-scale invasion. Following the fall of Phnom Penh on 7 January 1979, Vietnamese-backed rebel forces declared Pol Pot and the infamous Khmer Rouge to be overthrown and formed a government. However, fighting between the rival factions continued in the west of the country, forcing thousands of refugees to flee into neighbouring Thailand.

Concerned that an estimated army of 200,000 Vietnamese regulars in Kampuchea might turn their weapons on them, the Thai government requested US reconnaissance coverage of the area.

In total, five SR-71 sorties were flown in support of this request, the first by Majs Tom Keck and Tim Shaw in '979' on 17 February 1980. This was followed by Majs Rick Young and Russ Szcepanik, again in '979', on 3 May, Majs Gil Bertelson and Frank Stampf in '976' on 3 August, and Majs Bob Crowder and John Morgan in '960' on 22 November. Finally, Majs B C Thomas and Jay Reid completed this series of sorties, codenamed *Giant Scale II* by SAC, in '976' on 24 November.

Each round robin mission from Kadena covered approximately 6500 miles, and required three aerial refuellings – one over the Philippine Sea and the other two over the Gulf of Thailand. All five were PHOTINT missions, with the aircraft configured with an OBC unit in the nose and TEOCs in the chine bays. Four of the five sorties secured standard black and white imagery of the target area. However, the JCS directed that the cameras for the mission flown in '960' should be loaded with Kodak SO-131 camouflage detection film. It coloured healthy vegetation red and dead or dying vegetation in various shades of grey and white. This was used to gauge the probable yield of the rice crop, since Kampuchea had become a member of the United Nations in September 1980.

After processing, the imagery was forwarded to the DIA, where it enabled analysts to help plan the US contribution level to the food relief programme. The rest of the reconnaissance imagery collected during the other four sorties failed to reveal any large concentrations of Vietnamese troops or equipment along the Thai border, and after sanitising the photography, it was passed, via the US Embassy in Bangkok, to high-level officials in the Thai government.

GIANT COBRA AND *GIANT EXPRESS*

The Horn of Africa is an immensely important strategic location, 'guarding' the Red Sea approach to the Suez Canal and overlooking the 'oil arteries' of Saudi Arabia, Iraq, Oman, Kuwait, Djibouti and the United Arab Emirates as they fan out from the southern entrance to the Red Sea.

In August 1977, a war broke out between communist-governed Ethiopia and its neighbour Somalia. In November that same year, the Soviet Union began airlifting arms to Ethiopia, and these were backed-up by Cuban troops, sent by Fidel Castro. By March 1978, it was estimated that approximately 11,000 Cuban troops were 'in-country', and two Soviet generals were directing the ground war against Somalia.

Accordingly, the JCS directed that SAC should position a Kadena-based SR-71 to Diego Garcia, a small British-owned atoll in the Indian Ocean, and plan a round-robin PHOTINT reconnaissance mission over the area to monitor the extent of Soviet and Cuban presence. In response, the SRC prepared a track for such a sortie, and the JCS directed that the flight should launch on 12 March 1978.

However, the theatre situation changed dramatically shortly before the flight was scheduled to take place when Somalia suddenly withdrew its troops from Ethiopia and agreed to keep them out, provided that all foreign troops also consented to leave the region. As a result, the mission was cancelled prior to the SR-71 being positioned on the tiny island.

This event, however, proved to be a catalyst in the preparation of Diego Garcia to enable it to support SR-71 contingency operations in the Indian Ocean area. In just three weeks from mid-February 1978, an SR-71 shelter at Beale was dismantled, transported to and re-erected on Diego Garcia. The island was also provided with a water demineralisation plant, crew rations and a handful of 376th SW KC-135Qs with JP 7 fuel. The fragmentary order activating any such contingency operations in this theatre was initially codenamed *Giant Cobra*.

As the region experienced further political upheaval with the rise to power of Ayatollah Khomeini and his brand of Islamic fundamentalism in Iran and Soviet involvement in Afghanistan, it was decided to further bolster facilities on Diego Garcia in the event that the needs of national intelligence users required more extensive coverage of the area.

On 2 April 1979, the JCS directed SAC to create a permanent SR-71 fuel storage facility on Diego Garcia. Initially, two 50,000-gallon polyurethane fuel storage bladders were deployed and filled by ten Kadena-based KC-135Qs in an operation codenamed *Giant Ace*. On 1 May 1979, a follow-on fragmentary order codenamed *Giant Express* took cognisance of the deteriorating situation and included not only the Indian Ocean area, but also Africa and Southwest Asia as potential theatres of operation from Diego Garcia.

Further developments on the island by the US Navy, eventually freed up a 1.26 million gallon fuel tank for prospective SR-71 operations, this was filled with JP-7 delivered by ocean tanker.

During the summer of 1980, the JCS approved a plan to exercise the newly created SR-71 facilities. Consequently, on 1 July, Majs Bob Crowder and Don Emmons completed the 4-hr 24-minute flight in '962' to the island. The flight included three aerial refuellings – two from KC-135Qs operating from Kadena and a third from tankers that had been deployed a week earlier to Diego Garcia. The aircraft and crew returned to Kadena on 4 July, but despite validating the facilities and

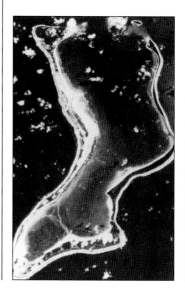

SR-71 '962' took this photograph of Diego Garcia, in the Indian Ocean, during the jet's deployment to the British-controlled atoll in early July 1980. It was prepared for SR-71 operations, but in the event no missions were ever undertaken from the atoll (*USAF*)

subsequent sorties being flown in the region, SR-71s never returned to the tropical island.

SOVIET UNION

Located on the far eastern extremity of the Soviet Union were two ports that were of considerable interest to the US Navy. Petropavlovsk, on the eastern coastline of the Kamchatka Peninsula, with the Sea of Okhotsk to the west and the northern Pacific on its east coast, is a desolate port almost hidden among ancient volcanoes and primeval birch forests. It was home to a large missile submarine base. Much further to the south, on the Sea of Japan, is Vladivostok, which was the USSR's largest naval base in the Pacific – both ports were extremely well defended by SA-5 SAMs and MiG-25 'Foxbat' fighters.

Thanks to the SR-71's HRR intelligence capabilities, the jet's utility increased considerably when it was agreed in the late 1970s that Det OL-KA would monitor submarine movements in these ports for the US Navy. These missions also provided an opportunity for the USAF to monitor missile and radar defences.

Such data had to be collected whilst the SR-71 was flying in international airspace off the Soviet coastline, utilising stand-off viewing. There were problems associated with performing these missions, however, as there were only limited track variations available for this type of stand-off sortie. A crew could fly up or down the coastline, or directly towards it and then break away to the left or right. An important part of the mission planning process for these flights was to develop ingenious flight profiles and tracks designed to keep Soviet defence controllers guessing as to the 'Habu's' intentions in order to stimulate the SIGINT environment.

Having closely monitored the comings and goings of SR-71s over a number of years as they deployed to and returned from Kadena, the Soviets were extremely familiar with their route. However, on 9 August 1977, Majs Al Cirino and Bruce Liebman departed Kadena in '976' for Beale, but their flight track was considerably different from all those followed in the past. For the first time, an operational mission was planned into the return flight home, enabling the aircraft to monitor important military facilities along the Kamchatka peninsula.

The next day, Majs Maury Rosenberg and Al Payne repeated this innovative idea in reverse, completing an operational mission in '960' during their positioning flight from Beale down to Kadena.

By early 1980, the mission planners had evolved another much more demanding piece of 'Habu' choreography that was guaranteed to get Soviet controllers very excited, thus provoking them into activating radars that would otherwise have remained dormant. At 0923 hrs local, Majs Tom Alison and J T Vida were airborne from Kadena in '972' for the flight back to Beale. Twenty minutes later, Majs Tom Keck and Tim Shaw launched '962' from Kadena as an airborne spare, just in case '972' had to abort. However, in the event all went exactly according to plan.

Meanwhile, Majs Bob Crowder and Don Emmons were roaring towards Kadena from Beale in '976', and they were just off the coast of Petropavlovsk as '972' rapidly approached from the south. Heading directly towards one another, and maintaining a reciprocal course, to aid

visual acquisition, both crews dumped fuel. They passed one another within ten seconds of their planned time. Tom Alison remembers the event as 'a spectacular experience, as Bob and Don passed us, head on, about 5000 ft below us at a closure rate of over Mach 6!' Not surprisingly, the operation triggered a series of atypical reactions from the region's numerous radar sites, and the ELINT collecting systems of both SR-71s and an RC-135 also sent to the area yielded a rich SIGINT harvest.

4 September 1980 witnessed another interesting piece of SR-71 deception. On this occasion, Majs Tom Alison and J T Vida were inbound to Kadena from Beale in '960'. At 0944 hrs, Majs Lee Shelton and Barry MacKean took off in '976' from Kadena and headed north. The two RSOs each completed a textbook piece of tri-sonic navigation, passing one another exactly on time off the coast of Vladivostok. After passing, '976' turned around and flew back at Kadena – it landed shortly after '960' had touched down. For those monitoring aircraft movements just off base on 'Habu Hill', it must have appeared that 'Black Magic' was in the air! One SR-71 gets airborne and two land back, minutes apart, two-and-a-half hours later.

By March 1984, Tom Alison, now a lieutenant colonel, was the commander at Det 1, and on the morning of 27 March 1984, Majs 'Stormy' Boudreaux and Ted Ross got airborne from Kadena in '964' and headed north-east towards Vladivostok. Lt Col Les Dyer and Maj Dan

As early as 1960, the Mikoyan-Gurevich Opytno-Konstruktorskoye Byuro (OKB design bureau) began developing a multi-role supersonic interceptor with, it was planned, the capability of defeating a new generation of high performance aerial threats then under development in the United States. The end results were the MiG-25 'Foxbat' and a later two-seat radical redesign in the form of the awesome MiG-31 'Foxhound'. The jet in this photograph is a MiG-25PD 'Foxbat-E' (*Yefim Gordon*)

Aircraft '972' taxies out to the holding area at Kadena. Sent to here during its final deployment between 19 July 1979 and 24 June 1980. '972' also set a speed record between New York and London on 1 September 1974. Retired in 1990, the jet is now on display in the Smithsonian Institution's Dulles Airport facility in Washington, DC (*Lindsay Peacock*)

Greenwood had launched earlier from Beale in '973', heading for Kadena, via Vladivostok. Codenamed *Busy Relay*, the two aircraft streaked towards each other from opposite directions, again at a closure speed of Mach 6, and only three miles apart. Boudreaux and Ross then turned right to follow Dyer and Greenwood south and west across South Korea, just south of the Demilitarised Zone. Yet again, the appearance of two SR-71s off Vladivostok generated another bumper SIGINT take.

Aircraft '964' undertook just two deployments to Kadena – the first between 15 February 1983 and 30 March 1984, and the second from 11 December 1984 through to 1 August 1985. Today, the aircraft is on display in the SAC Museum in Omaha, Nebraska (*USAF*)

CONFRONTATION WITH NORTH KOREA

A total of three reconnaissance sorties were flown over North Korea by *Oxcart* pilots in 1968, but their short-lived efforts passed to SAC as a long-term role in early 1968 when the 9th SRW's OL-8 (OL-RK) inherited the CIA's facilities at Kadena. The principal objectives of these Western Pacific missions was to identify any build up in communist forces north of the DMZ. Most of operational objectives were achieved from international airspace by either flying off the North Korean coast or over the DMZ itself.

Such missions were launched to satisfy the requirements specified primarily by the Commander-in-Chief, Pacific on behalf of the intelligence users who operated under his jurisdiction, the most important of whom were Commander, United States Forces, Korea (COMUSK), Commander-in-Chief, Pacific Fleet (CINCPACFLT) and the Intelligence Center Pacific (ICPAC).

The justification for designating this region as a principal area of operations was based upon the fact that by 1977, North Korea had an army of 450,000 men (by mid-1978, the DIA and CIA believed that this number had increased to between 550,000 and 600,000), which made it the fifth largest in the world. In addition, the country's unpredictable dictator Kim Il Sung was committed to the reunification of the peninsula under his form of communism.

Adm Maurice Weisner, who at that time was CINCPACFLT, believed that given the sophistication of North Korea's weaponry and the level of training undertaken by its troops, Kim Il Sung could order an attack across the DMZ at anytime.

(*text continues on page 76*)

Groundcrew technicians scrutinise '976' one last time before Majs Tom Alison and J T Vida taxi to the runway at the beginning of a 3.8-hour sortie to monitor North Korea on 11 July 1977 (*Toshiki Kudo via Robert F Dorr*)

1
**A-12 '77855' of the 1129th Special Activities
Squadron, Kadena air base, Okinawa,
October 1967**

2
**A-12 Article Number 127 (60-6930) of the 1129th
Special Activities Squadron, Groom Dry Lake,
late 1963**

3
AT-12 Article Number 124 (60-6927) of the 1129th
Special Activities Squadron, Groom Dry Lake,
1965

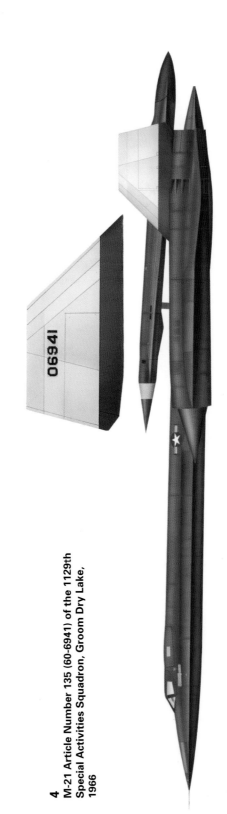

4
M-21 Article Number 135 (60-6941) of the 1129th
Special Activities Squadron, Groom Dry Lake,
1966

5
YF-12A Article Number 1001 (60-6934),
Edwards North Base, 1964

6
YF-12C (SR-71) Article Number 2002 (60-6937),
NASA, Edwards AFB, 1972

7
SR-71A Article Number 2018 (64-17967) of the 9th
SRW's Det 1, Kadena air base, Okinawa, late 1977

8
SR-71A Article Number 2025 (64-17974) of the
9th SRW's OL-8, Kadena air base, Okinawa,
September 1968

9
SR-71A Article Number 2029 (64-17978) of the
9th SRW's OL-KA, Kadena air base, Okinawa,
July 1972

10
SR-71A Article Number 2026 (64-17975) of the
9th SRW's OL-8, Kadena air base, Okinawa,
June 1969

11
SR-71A Article Number 2013 (64-17962) of the
9th SRW's Det 1, Kadena air base, Okinawa,
January 1990

12
SR-71B Article 2008 (64-17957) of the 9th SRW.
Beale AFB, 1967

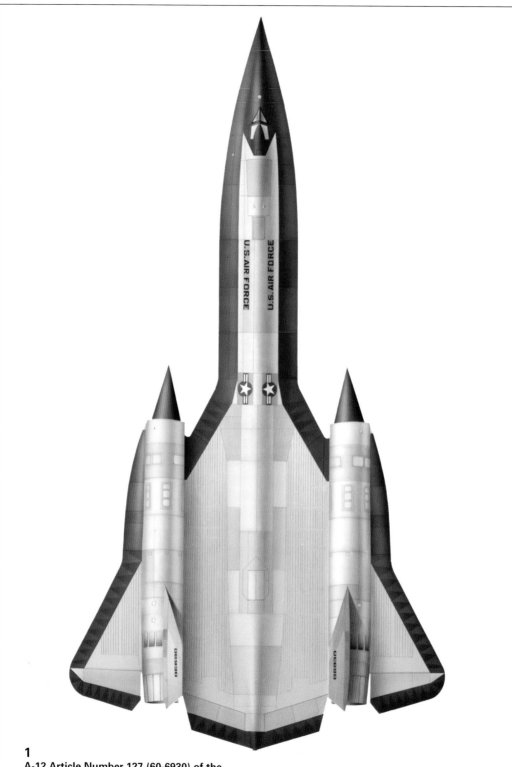

1
A-12 Article Number 127 (60-6930) of the
1129th Special Activities Squadron, Groom
Dry Lake, late 1963

2
SR-71A Article Number 2025 (64-17974) of
the 9th SRW's OL-8, Kadena air base,
Okinawa, September 1968

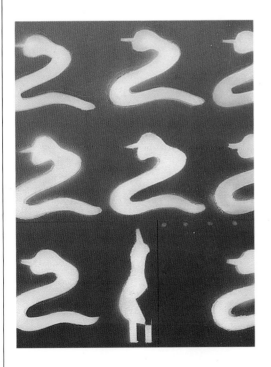

Majs Al Cirino and Bruce Leibman accelerate down the Kadena runway in '979' at the start of a Peacetime Aerial Reconnaissance Operations Program (PAROP) sortie to monitor North Korea on 15 March 1977. The aircraft was equipped with a TROC, two OOCs and its nose-mounted SLAR. This mission was aborted due to a mechanical problem, and crew recovered back to Kadena after 2.7 flight hours (*Steve Myatt*)

On 19 September 1977, the first in a series of SR-71 night-monitoring PAROP sorties of North Korea was flown by aircraft '960' (*USAF*)

He therefore requested that the JCS authorise SAC to increase the number of SR-71 monitoring sorties to the area from eight to twelve per month. The SRC scheduled the SR-71 to be configured with cameras on two of the sorties so as to collect Radar Intelligence (RADINT) using its HRR. ELINT would be gathered on the remaining ten missions. The PHOTINT provided a reference base for intelligence specialists to use when interpreting the HRR imagery.

North Korea's propensity to re-locate or re-enforce its military units and installations along the DMZ after dark prompted a further request from US theatre commanders that these SR-71 'indications and warning' sorties be conducted at night. This was communicated by the JCS to the SRC, and at 2105 hrs, on 19 September 1977, Majs Jack Veth and (RSO) Bill Keller left Kadena in '960'. They returned 4.1 hrs later, having completed the first night monitoring sortie of North Korea.

Four additional RADINT/ELINT night sorties of North Korea were completed before year-end (27 September by Majs Kinego and Elliott in aircraft '967', 16 and 25 November by Lt Col Alison and Maj Vida in '967' and '960', and finally on 13 December by Majs Carpenter and Murphy, again in aircraft '960').

The crews that flew these missions were, however, less than impressed by their nocturnal forays, noting that the aircraft's cockpit lighting was uneven, causing reflections that made monitoring instrumentation extremely difficult and potentially dangerous – especially during the descent phase to rendezvous with a tanker. This situation could be further complicated by a lack of horizon. Such conditions could trigger vertigo and pilot disorientation, leading to the loss of an aircraft.

Therefore, after the first two sorties flown in September, the mission profile was amended and the number of aerial refuellings reduced from two to one. The impact of this decision was to also reduce the number of passes made through the sensitive area from two to one, which in turn also reduced the flight time needed to execute such missions from just under four-and-a-half hours to two-and-a-half hours.

Finally, in a further move to alleviate the onset of vertigo, the missions were flown at Mach 2.8 and bank angles restricted to a maximum of 35 degrees. This problem was finally rectified in 1982 when the cockpit lighting was improved and Peripheral Vision Horizon Display (PVHD) units were fitted in the SR-71. These units projected a thin red line of light across the jet's

instrument panel that created an artificial horizon that responded to changes in pitch and roll, duplicating the behaviour of a natural horizon.

In April 1981, SR-71 flights began collecting ELINT 'cuts' and other raw data on a suspected SA-2 site which was under construction on the island of Choc Tarrie in an estuary near the western end of Korea's DMZ. In July and August of that year, Maj Maury Rosenberg and Capt E D McKim flew several passes over Korea to check on the progress of the Choc Tarrie's site. Before each flight, Det 1's intelligence officer briefed crews about the most recent developments, since it was increasingly apparent that the North Koreans were about to embark upon another 'adventure in belligerence'.

On 25 August, Majs Nevin Cunningham and Geno Quist climbed into '967' for a similar two-loop sortie of the 'Z' area. Although it was a clear day over the target area, the primary sensor for this four-hour mission was the SLAR. During their fourth and final pass over the DMZ, the crew realised that they were still carrying excess fuel, so Cunningham flicked his fuel dump switch in quick Morse-Code bursts, which spelled out a four-letter expletive for the benefit of the ground trackers who were attempting to follow the SR-71 visually. Their humour was lost on the enemy, but it brought lots of laughs back at the 'Habu' bar at Kadena.

The next morning, Rosenberg and McKim were briefed for their mission, which entailed three passes along the DMZ. Once again they were briefed about the 'suspected' SA-2 site, and Rosenberg asked the intelligence officer 'Who determines when a suspected site becomes a confirmed site?' He was told that the DIA made the final call. The pilot replied, 'So what do we have to do before we can confirm it? See a missile?' 'Well, that would surely help', answered the intelligence officer!

Rosenberg and McKim launched in '976' on their 'Z' sortie and headed for their first aerial refuelling. After tanking, they flew through the Straits of Formosa and made their first high pass from west to east along Korea's DMZ. They then turned south and flew down the east coast of South Korea towards their second refuelling. Thereafter, they reversed course and after reaching operational altitude off the west coast of South Korea, they repeated their west-to-east run across the DMZ.

Coasting out to the east, Rosenberg made a right and left 90-270 degree turn, which put '976' on an east-to-west pass. While approaching the western side of Korea at Mach 3 and 77,000 ft, McKim remarked that he was getting some DEF System activity, and that everything was turned on'. In the next breath, the RSO exclaimed, 'Wow! It looks like we've had a launch'. Maury accelerated to Mach 3.2 and told McKim, 'I see a contrail! I'll be damned, it's coming right at us'. Maury made a slight turn to the left to turn away from the rising contrail, which took them further into South Korean airspace, and watched as the SA-2 missed by a good two miles, exploding behind and to the right of them at about 80,000 ft.

On 26 August 1981, Maj Maury Rosenberg (second from left) and RSO Capt E D McKim had two SA-2 SAMs fired at them by North Korea whilst flying aircraft '976' (*Maury Rosenberg*)

Always mindful of the sensitivity of such sorties, US authorities monitored these SR-71 flights very closely. Almost as soon as '976' came off track, McKim received an encoded HF message from *Sky King* concerning the track deviation. There was no mention of the hostile missile firing. The RSO responded with the appropriate messages, but found that there was no specific coded message that could be sent alluding to the missile incident. As a result of this mission, a coded message format was later added should a crew find themselves in similar circumstances. It was not until the 'Habu' crew arrived back on 'the Rock' that they could inform the staff that they had been shot at.

The incident was of such importance that a coded message was despatched to all interested agencies, including the National Security Council. Secretary of Defense Casper Weinberger informed President Ronald Reagan of the firing, after which a series of high-level briefings followed. Deputy Secretary of Defense Frank Carlucci recalled that President Reagan was 'furious' over the incident. Meanwhile, State Department spokesman Dean Fischer said, 'The Reagan Administration roundly denounces this act of lawlessness', adding that the attack violated 'accepted norms of international behavior'.

Despite faultless photographic evidence of the North Korean SAM battery firing at a jet over South Korea, Kim Il Sung's government denied the missile charge. While the diplomatic rhetoric continued, Det 1 was told to move the reconnaissance track flown by the SR-71 further south. Six days later, Majs Nev Cunningham and Geno Quist flew a typical four-hour, two-loop sortie along the DMZ in '976', with little reaction.

Majs B C Thomas and Jay Reid arrived at Kadena during this period of high-level interest in Det 1's activities. On 26 September, Deputy SECDEF Frank Carlucci visited the island and was briefed on operations. He was also shown an SR-71 for the first time. Carlucci met with the 'Habu' crewmembers and explained that the DMZ route package had been moved further to the south for the moment, but that they would return to their former DMZ routes after 'certain preparations' were made. He did not explain what those preparations were, but seemed angry about the attempted shoot-down. Carlucci added that the US government viewed such hostile actions with serious concern, and

Early night-monitoring sorties of North Korea in the SR-71 proved to be quite challenging for the crews involved due to the jet's uneven cockpit lighting. Reflections also made it extremely difficult for the pilot and RSO to monitor their instrumentation (*Lockheed*)

emphasised that the President would not stand for a repeat of such an aggressive act.

On Friday, 2 October, Thomas and Reid flew '967' on a sortie along the eastern coast of China, North Korea and the USSR. They reported an unusual massing of ships off the coast of North Korea. The next day, Lt Gen Robert Mathis (Assistant Vice Chief of Staff) held a special briefing for the Det's crewmembers to tell them about four special category missions that were to be flown on routes which would follow the same triple-pass track that Maury Rosenberg had flown when he was shot at on 26 August. He emphasised that the timing would be extremely important, and that the 'Habu' had to be over the earlier mission's firing point within 30 seconds of their mission's pre-planned timing. Timing control triangles would be built into the flight track after the second aerial refuelling to ensure that its precise timing constraints were met.

One of the pilots asked why timing was so important. Gen Mathis explained that 'Wild Weasel' anti-radar strike aircraft would be poised to hit any North Korean SAM site within 60 seconds of a launch against the SR-71. The time constraint would ensure that the strike aircraft were headed in the right direction at the moment a missile was launched. President Reagan had personally approved the plan.

Operational sorties to the DMZ continued to be flown along the amended route until 26 October 1981, when, following extensive mission planning and detailed briefings, Majs B C Thomas and Jay Reid took-off from Kadena on time in '975'. All four of these high-priority missions were ground-spared as insurance against an abort of the primary aircraft. Thomas recalled:

'We had to employ the timing triangles to lose a few minutes of "pad" – we were also delayed with the tanker all the way to the end of the second aerial refuelling for the same reason. We flew over the critical point within ten seconds of the designated time, feeling very proud of ourselves.

'We all felt that it was this mission, which had such importance attached to it, and all of the preparation that had gone into it, to be the pinnacle of our professional efforts. Even though there was no firing, I experienced the greatest sense of well being knowing that we did the whole operation "exactly as

On 21 April 1989, aircraft '974' became the last 'Habu' to be lost prior to the *Senior Crown* programme being axed. Here, the sad remains of '974' break the surface during recovery operations off the Philippines conducted by the US Navy salvage vessel USS *Beaufort* (*USAF*)

planned". I must admit that I'd hoped that the North Koreans would fire at us. Their missile capability never bothered us, and I believe that it is fair for me to say that by immediately smashing their launch facility, our national resolve would have been most graphically demonstrated.'

For whatever reason, the North Koreans chose not to launch a missile at this or any other trawling mission, and B C Thomas (and all who had preceded him) recovered safely after his four-hour flight.

ANOTHER LOST 'HABU'

After more than 21 years of operating from Kadena, and 17 years without the loss of a single 'Habu' from any location, '974' crashed near the Philippines on 21 April 1989. Lt Col Dan House and Maj Blair Bozek had departed Kadena and headed 'straight out' to speed and altitude without a top-off aerial refuelling, ready to perform a routine stand-off sortie along the coast of Southeast Asia.

After House levelled off at 75,000 ft and Mach 3, the aircraft began yawing to the left. It did not appear to be a typical unstart and the inlet had not re-cycled. He continued to monitor his instruments, and soon the left engine's gauges were winding down. He told Bozek that the left engine had quit. By then there was no RPM, EGT or oil pressure, and the pressure gauges for the A and L hydraulic systems indicated 'zero'. The left engine had seized. It had been a surprisingly gentle process, but it was nonetheless an immediate abort item.

Consequently, the crew began to plan for a diversionary landing, while following-up on their 'engine out' procedures. At that point, the right engine went through four unstarts, during which another of the flight control's SAS channels failed, leaving them with only one out of six. As the jet lost speed and altitude, it entered a series of lateral gyrations that threatened to take the aeroplane beyond the limits of its flight envelope. Now at 400 knots and 15,000 ft, the crew turned left into the dead engine and decided to attempt an emergency diversion into Clark AFB, in the Philippines. Moments later their plight deteriorated still further when the pressure gauge for the B hydraulic system began to fluctuate.

Now searching desperately for anywhere to put the 'Habu' down, House noted that the B hydraulic system had now dropped to zero – he was holding the aircraft on full left rudder, and '974' began wrapping up to the right very rapidly. It was time to leave.

Both crewmembers ejected safely and the stricken 'Habu' crashed, inverted into the sea. House and Bozek were subsequently rescued by two Philippino fishermen and then airlifted by an HH-53 Super Jolly Green Giant helicopter to Clark AFB. The shattered remains of '974' were eventually recovered from the depths of the Philippine Sea by the US Navy's dedicated salvage vessel USS *Beaufort*.

Both Majs Dan House and (RSO) Blair Bozek safely ejected from '974' before it tumbled into the Philippine Sea – note the ejector seat rail to the right of the photograph (*USAF*)

MIDDLE EAST AND SHUTDOWN

In the face of a resurgence in Islamic Fundamentalism, the pro-US Shah of Iran was driven into exile on 16 January 1979. Anti-American feeling in the country grew progressively worse, and when, in October, the exiled Shah was operated on in a New York hospital and diagnosed as suffering from cancer, Ayatollah Khalkhali urged Muslims to 'drag him out of his hospital bed and dismember him'. Worse was to follow on 4 November, when the cleric's fanatical followers stormed the US Embassy in Tehran, brushed aside Marine Corps guards and occupied the building, taking nearly 100 embassy staff hostage.

Over the next few weeks, non-US citizens were released, and on 25 April 1980, in an operation codenamed *Eagle Claw* mounted by America's crack Delta Force, an attempt was made to free the remaining 53 diplomatic hostages. Alas, the audacious raid went catastrophically wrong, and eight would-be rescuers were killed in the desert 200 miles southeast of their objective. For President Jimmy Carter it was an international humiliation.

The collection of intelligence concerning the hostages was codenamed *Snowbird*, and this continued after *Eagle Claw*, as did military planning for another possible rescue effort, codenamed *Double Star*. But the only substantial intelligence assets available to the US after the botched April rescue attempt were satellites. However, various options were contemplated, including leaflet dropping, although it is still not apparent what such an activity would have achieved.

Subsequently, on 26 June 1980, a feasibility study and cost estimate schedule was requested from Lockheed ADP to provide an SR-71 with such a leaflet capability. This was provided by Lockheed on 9 July, wherein it was envisaged that the system would be designed for internal installation in the existing TROC camera bay. Capable of dispensing 10,000 leaflets, the system was activated by air-charged initiators and powered by 1000-lb force actuators. Four systems, it noted, would be built, with two being flight-tested and two made available for operational use at a cost of $2.2 million. Nothing ever came of the idea.

The other plan involved American use of certain airfields near Tehran, from where a second rescue attempt would be launched. However, when it was learned that the Iranians might be attempting to block the runways at these airfields, the JCS requested that action be initiated to investigate the feasibility of an SR-71 overflying these locations and using its HRR to define such obstructions.

In response, an SR-71 mission was flown over Condron army airfield in White Sands, New Mexico, on the night of 27 June when its runway was clear. A second sortie was flown over the same airfield on the night of

During its fourth deployment to Kadena, between 24 June 1980 and 7 June 1982, '976' sported the 9th SRW insignia on its twin tail units. (*Toshiki Kudo via Robbie Shaw*)

An SR-71 take-off was always a noisy affair, with the aircraft's J58 turbojets in full afterburner producing distinctive shock patterns in the aircraft's exhaust flame. At low speeds and altitudes, the 'Habu's' engine configuration was relatively inefficient, being optimised for high-speed, high-altitude cruising. Under optimum conditions, clever intake and nacelle design, using the variable intake spikes and bleed/bypass systems, allowed much greater efficiency. A veteran of a number of deployments to Kadena between April 1969 and 30 June 1988, '975' departs the base on a 'Habu' mission in late 1981. This aircraft has been on display in the March AFB museum in California since February 1990 (*USAF*)

30 June after a combination of vehicles, steel drums, tyres, rocks, wire cable, logs and dirt piles had been left along the runway's edge. A qualified Photo Interpreter then completed an analysis of the SR-71's HRR imagery to ascertain what level of obstruction could be detected.

In a memo for the record, classified Top Secret and dated 9 July 1980, it was decided that the CAPRE system then equipping the SR-71 fleet was 'capable of detection of runway obstructions expected to be of concern for project *Double Star*'.

On 3 November 1980, Maj Gen James B Vaught of the JCS submitted a Top Secret memo to the Joint Reconnaissance Centre, entitled 'SR-71 Mission Request'. It set out the following points;

'Request consideration be given to conducting several SR-71 surveillance missions of the Persian Gulf during the next 3-6 weeks.

'1. Purpose of mission is to determine locations of major oil rig concentrations and typical flow pattern of Gulf shipping to assist in selection of low level air penetration routes.

'2. Recognise that missions could raise Soviet/Iran/Middle East speculation. However, given irregular scheduling, direct association with any US military planning will probably be low. On the other hand, periodic SR-71 missions would provide "reason" for increased tanker support in the area prior to the execution of any US military contingency action.'

Despite the request, immediate action wasn't forthcoming, and Det 1 was not tasked to perform these sorties – operations into this area would have to wait for another seven years. So, with the request on the 'backburner', diplomatic efforts intensified, and finally came to fruition

on 21 January 1981, when the remaining 52 hostages were released after a marathon 444 days in captivity.

IRAN-IRAQ WAR

On 24 September 1980, a simmering border war between Iraq and Iran flared into full-scale hostilities when Iraqi troops and tanks invaded Iran. Their dawn attack set the world's largest oil refinery at Abadan ablaze. The Iraqis quickly seized the port of Khorramshahr, and they advanced ten miles into Iranian territory. Despite initial successes by the Iraqi Army, the conflict quickly turned into a stalemate, with both sides digging in and fighting a long and bloody trench war not too dissimilar to the battles fought in Flanders and Verdun some 65 years earlier.

Both the USSR and the US made it clear that neither side would get involved, and that they would remain 'strictly neutral'. However, the US intelligence community fully understood how easy it would be for Iran to exploit the 'oil pressure point.'

On 24 May 1984, two Iranian aircraft attacked an oil tanker off the Saudi Arabian coast. As East-West countercharges continued over the next few years, Iraq's jets attacked the key Iranian oil terminals on Kharg Island. The Iranians in turn attacked oil-laden supertankers bound for the West from Kuwait, Saudi Arabia and Bahrain. To offer greater protection to these unarmed vessels, the US government planned to 'reflag' such tankers as American ships, and to escort them through the 'choke point' at the Straits of Hormuz.

On 18 May 1987, two Iraqi Air Force Mirages F 1s, each carrying an AM.39 Exocet anti-ship missile, locked onto a surface target in the waters north of Bahrain. They both fired their sea-skimming weapons 12 miles from the target – fortunately, the warhead on one of the missiles failed to explode. The other Exocet, however, worked with devastating effect, hitting the frigate

Aircraft '958' was the first SR-71 to be equipped with a Digital Automatic Flight Inlet Control System (DAFICS). The jet performed its second, and last, Det 1 deployment between 11 June 1985 (when it was flown in by Majs Jack Madison and Bill Orcutt) and 5 April 1986 (when it was flown out by Majs Duane Noll and Tom Veltri). It is seen here taxiing out for its first operational mission of the deployment on 24 June 1985, with Majs Noll and Charlie Morgan at the controls. This aircraft resides in the Robbins AFB museum in Georgia (*Toshiki Kudo via Robbie Shaw*)

Prior to '958' being rotated back to Beale in July 1981 following its first stint with Det 1, the jet was painted with tail art that featured a white Habu snake (*via Author*)

USS *Stark* and killing 28 sailors. The vessel was left disabled and burning. President Reagan immediately demanded an Iraqi explanation for the attack, which a Baghdad spokesman said was due to the pilots identifying the frigate as Iranian.

The situation in the Persian Gulf continued to escalate, and on 22 July 1987, Majs Mike Smith and Doug Soifer were the first to fly four very long non-stop reconnaissance missions from Kadena into the region. Majs Ed Yeilding and Curt Osterheld backed them up as spare crew in '967'. As the primary crew stepped from the PSD van toward their jet – '975' – Col Tom Alison and Lt Col Tom Henichek (the Det commander and ops officer) informed them both that '975's' ANS had not checked out properly, and that they would have to take '967' instead. Yeilding and Osterheld would follow in '975' after its ANS problem was resolved.

Above
On 22 July 1987, Majs Mike Smith and Doug Soifer were the first of three crews to fly a long endurance mission from Kadena to the Persian Gulf (*USAF*)

The 11-hour sortie would involve two refuellings on the outbound leg and three on the return. As Smith and Soifer approached their second aerial rendezvous they called Yeilding and Osterheld, who were two hours behind in '967', and told them that everything was progressing well, and that their services would not be required that day. The most distant second and third tankings were to be carried out by three KC-10s before and after '967' had flown over the 'cuckoo's nest'. The KC-10s were able to extend their range by 'buddy' refuelling each other. As a result of this, Smith was able to take on distant pre- and post-target split-onloads from the two tankers during each refuelling.

The cloud cover had been almost continually undercast since they left Kadena, and as '967' was equipped with Technical Objective Cameras and an Optical Bar Panoramic Camera, it looked as if the mission could prove to be a very expensive failure. After much 'gas guzzling', they headed out 'hot and high' to boom the Gulf region. Suddenly the

The RSO's view-sight display can be seen at the top of this photograph, with the Synthetic Aperture Radar (SAR) display screen immediately below it. When re-equipped with SAR, the SR-71 was used extensively to obtain extremely high-resolution imagery of target areas obscured by cloud (*Curt Osterheld*)

Left
The RSO's right cockpit panel, which housed the Astro-Inertial Navigation System controls and display (*Curt Osterheld*)

undercast disappeared and conditions were perfect for their high-resolution cameras to do some of their finest work. Their fifth and final refuelling – at night – was completed ten hours after take-off. It was complicated by the failure of one of the KC-10's boom lights, which made proper formation flying (in the close-in contact position) difficult. Despite that added strain to an already tiring flight (at the near limit of the aircraft and aircrew's flight duration), Smith landed an almost 'zero write-up' 'Habu' back at Kadena after a flight lasting 11 hours and 12 minutes.

On 9 August, Majs Terry Pappas and John Manzi left Kadena in '975' and headed out for the first of many aerial refuellings. After clearing the first tanker, they climbed and accelerated toward Southeast Asia and then on past the south of India toward a second refuelling, and their distant target area. Five hours after take-off, they neared the collection area in the Persian Gulf. Everything had worked exactly as planned, and soon they were heading eastbound on their long trip back to Kadena. It had not been a simple, straightforward mission by any stretch of the imagination, however. Bad weather during two of the refuellings and a boom malfunction dictated that Pappas had to maintain his contact position with the tankers for three-and-a-half hours during the mission.

To make matters worse, nine hours into the sortie he became temporarily blinded by the combined effects of pure oxygen and an overheat condition that had affected his 'moon suit's' faceplate. The simple task of reading his instruments became almost impossible without opening his visor, but such action was out of the question due to the greater dangers of decompression and hypoxia. Pappas recalls that by squinting hard he could produce tears, and the moisture revived his vision enough to continue the mission. He finally completed the sortie with a smooth night landing back at Kadena after flying for more than 11 hours.

Later in the summer of 1987, US intelligence discovered that the Iranians had acquired land-based 'Silkworm' (HY-2) anti-ship missiles from China. The weapon had a maximum range of about 60 miles, and employed active radar homing to locate its target. In September 1987, the Iranians began launching the missiles from the Al Faw peninsula at Kuwaiti oil terminals some 50 miles away. Initially, the weapons missed their targets and fell on uninhabited parts of the coastline, but on 22 October a Silkworm slammed into a Kuwaiti oil loading facility at Sea Island. The 1100-lb warhead caused extensive damage and triggered a major fire. Just four days after this attack Majs Warren McKendree and Randy Shelhorse completed their first Persian Gulf sortie in aircraft '967'.

Utilising surveillance information gathered from these flights and by satellite, US intelligence was able to determine the most likely positions from where the future deployment of Iranian 'Silkworms' could threaten the Kuwaiti oil terminals. An expert in decoys employed as a civil servant by the Naval Research Laboratory in Washington, DC devised a simple and cost effective solution to the problem by placing large corner reflectors on barges. Utilising the available imagery, these barges were then anchored between the likely launch sites and the potential targets.

On 7 December the Iranians launched a 'Silkworm' against a Kuwaiti oil pumping station. The decoy worked as planned and the missile struck one of the barge-mounted reflectors, the weapon's short-fuse delay detonating the warhead and blowing the unit off the barge. The

The view from the RSO's 'office window' at 85,000 ft (*Marta Bohn-Meyer*)

'Silkworm's target was unscathed, no one was injured in the attack and no further HY-2s were launched against the oil terminals.

Majs Dan House and Blair Bozek completed the last of these long-duration, high-priority missions in aircraft '974' on 30 April 1988. In addition to revealing the presence of Iranian 'Silkworms', the sorties had also gathered extensive intelligence on the vast array of military equipment in the region. Such imagery allowed US intelligence services were able to forewarn the US Navy of the 'Silkworm' threat, and diplomats were able to bring pressure to bear on Iran. The SR-71 had again carried out its mission in a distant part of the world.

In earlier times, the crews would surely have received Distinguished Flying Crosses for these unique and important sorties, but these flights were being flown at the very time when the USAF Chief of Staff Gen Larry Welch and other key SR-71 detractors were undermining the *Senior Crown* programme because of costs. The last thing they wanted were 'Habu Heroes'. Therefore, the crews were only awarded Air Medals.

SHUTDOWN

As the US disengaged itself from Vietnam and with the 1973 Middle East crisis over, the number of unit-authorised SR-71s also declined. By 1977, the number of Primary Authorised Aircraft, stood at just six jets, and funding was reduced proportionally. Since the SR-71 was primarily an image-gathering platform (PHOTINT and RADINT), it lost support from the National Intelligence Committee, which had become increasingly supportive of satellite-generated imagery. Having therefore lost much of the support of this powerful constituency, the *Senior Crown* programme had to be funded in its entirety by the USAF, despite being tasked by many agencies (particularly the US Navy) to support a variety of their theatre intelligence gathering requirements.

Even senior officers in HQ SAC had become hostile toward *Senior Crown* because SR-71 costs pulled on the purse strings of the command's

During the late 1980s, low visibility markings became the order of the day. Here, '979' is seen on final approach during its fifth, and final, deployment to Kadena – it was also one on the shortest, staying for just over a month, and completing seven operational missions in that time, including one inbound (3 July 1988) and one outbound (12 August 1988) from the island (*Toshiki Kudo via Robbie Shaw*)

funding, which was also required to cover its missile, bomber and tanker missions. Although SAC's SIOP needed SIGINT to keep it up to date, the SR-71 was not capable of gathering long on-station samples of this material like the RC-135 and U-2R fleet. Therefore, the loss of its SAC patronage left *Senior Crown* increasingly vulnerable.

To survive continued budget raids, the SR-71's utility was

improved, with the aircraft flying longer missions over many parts of the world – including from Detachment 4, established at RAF Mildenhall, in Suffolk, England. However, in order for the aircraft to compete with satellites, it had long been acknowledged even within the programme itself that the SR-71 needed to undergo a series of sensor updates, not least of which was an air-to-ground data-link system that provided the platform with a 'near real-time capability'. This, however, was not to materialise until after the bulk of the SR-71 fleet had been deactivated.

On 25 September 1989, Majs Don Watkins and Bob Fowlkes got airborne at 0910 hrs in '962' and completed what was to be the last SR-71 operational mission flown from Kadena. The second half of 1989 blew the structure of the Cold War away, as a gigantic political hurricane tore its way across eastern Europe and the Soviet Union, uprooting in its wake political leaders, institutions and establishments alike.

The scramble by western political leaders to 'cash-in' the so-called 'peace-dividend' in readiness for a promised 'New World Order' was as rapid as it was obscene – and, as history was to subsequently prove, equally as short-sighted. Despite intense lobbying by those involved directly and indirectly with the *Senior Crown* programme, all operational flights throughout the world ceased on 30 September 1989 when those who controlled and allocated the budget refused to commit further funding from the beginning of the new fiscal year.

With Det 1's SR-71 compliment having been reduced from two to just one aircraft on 12 August 1988, the ramifications for '962' – the aircraft that had arrived on 9 June 1989 following the loss of '974' on 21 April 1989 – meant that it completed 16 Functional Check and Crew Proficiency Flights from 28 August until 18 January 1990. The last flight of an SR-71 from Kadena occurred three days later on 21 January, when Majs Steve Grzebiniak and Jim Greenwood ferried '962' back to Beale. This sortie brought to a close nearly 22 years of 'Habu' activity by the Far East detachment.

On 21 January 1990, aircraft '962' became the last SR-71 to leave Kadena following the premature shutdown of the *Senior Crown* programme. This creative piece of tail art says it all. Significantly, the aircraft is now on display at the Imperial War Museum at Duxford, and as such, is the only SR-71 to be housed in a museum outside America (*USAF via Don Emmons*)

With the invaluable cooperation of Beale's base commander, Lockheed photographer Eric Schulzinger composed and took this historic masterpiece in February 1990. The SR-71 at the back is the hybrid SR-71C pilot trainer. Its rear section came from a retired YF-12A that was mated to a static test fore-body. It was constructed following the loss of '957' – one of only two two-seat SR-71B trainers. It handled like a dog and seldom flew (*Lockheed*)

APPENDICES

APPENDIX 1

BLACK SHIELD MISSIONS

Date number	Mission	Target	Pilot	Article number
31/5/67	BSX001	North Vietnam	Vojvodich	131
10/6/67	BSX003	North Vietnam	Weeks	131
20/6/67	BX6705	North Vietnam	Layton	127
30/6/67	BX6706	North Vietnam	Weeks	129
13/7/67	BX6708	North Vietnam	Collins	127
19/7/67	BX6709	North Vietnam	Sullivan	131
20/7/67	BX6710	North Vietnam	Collins	129
21/8/67	BX6716	North Vietnam	Vojvodich	131
31/8/67	BX6718	North Vietnam	Layton	127
16/9/67	BX6722	North Vietnam	Weeks	129
17/9/67	BX6723	North Vietnam	Collins	131
4/10/67	BX6725	North Vietnam	Collins	127
6/10/67	BX6727	North Vietnam	Murray	131
15/10/67	BX6728	North Vietnam	Collins	131
18/10/67	BX6729	North Vietnam	Murray	129
28/10/67	BX6732	North Vietnam	Sullivan	131
29/10/67	BX6733	North Vietnam	Murray	127
30/10/67	BX6734	North Vietnam	Sullivan	129
8/12/67	BX6737	Cambodia	Vojvodich	131
10/12/67	BX6738	Cambodia/Laos	Layton	131
15/12/67	BX6739	North Vietnam	Vojvodich	127
16/12/67	BX6740	North Vietnam	Layton	131
4/1/68	BX6842	North Vietnam	Layton	127
5/1/68	BX6843	North Vietnam	Weeks	131
26/1/68	BX6847	North Korea	Weeks	131
16/2/68	BX6851	North Vietnam	Collins	127
19/2/68	BX6853	North Korea	Murray	127
8/3/68	BX6856	North Vietnam	Vojvodich	127
6/5/68	BX6858	North Korea	Layton	127

APPENDIX 2

SR-71 DEPLOYMENTS TO KADENA

Serial number	Deployment date	Redeployment date
64-17958	17/7/80 (H)	16/7/81 (H)
	11/6/85 (H)	5/4/86 (H)
64-17960	10/8/77 (H)	23/6/79 (H)
	4/9/80 (H)	15/7/81 (H)
	12/11/83 (H)	20/11/83
64-17961	18/8/72	7/6/73
	16/8/74	21/7/76
64-17962	18/9/68	25/4/69
	6/6/73	20/8/74
	22/6/79 (H)	24/6/80 (H)
	9/6/89 (H)	21/1/90 (last SR-71 out)
64-17963	21/8/72	13/6/73
	13/8/74	16/7/76
64-17964	15/2/83 (H)	30/3/84 (H)
	11/12/84 (H)	1/8/85 (H)
64-17967	14/8/77	3/8/79
	16/7/81 (H)	30/6/82
	4/4/86 (H)	20/11/87 (H)
64-17968	10/6/71	19/8/72
	12/6/73	14/8/74
	31/7/85 (H)	14/5/87 (H)
64-17969	24/9/69	10/5/70 (crashed in Thailand)
64-17970	15/9/68	22/4/69
64-17971	18/4/69	1/10/69
	14/8/72	10/6/73
	26/11/74	14/7/76
64-17972	30/9/69	11/6/71
	9/6/73	17/8/74
	17/7/76	19/7/70 (H)
	19/7/79 (H)	24/6/80 (H)
64-17973	27/9/69	8/6/71
64-17974	13/3/68	16/9/68
	3/10/69	14/6/71
	19/11/87 (H)	21/4/89 (crashed into the Philippine Sea)
64-17975	24/4/69	22/10/69
	18/12/70	17/6/71
	11/8/72	12/8/77
	12/8/77	20/7/70 (H)
	14/7/80 (H)	17/2/83 (H)
	13/5/87 (H)	30/6/88 (H)
64-17976	11/3/68	13/9/68
	19/8/74	30/1/75
	20/7/76	9/8/77 (H)
	24/6/80 (H)	7/6/82
	19/11/83 (H)	13/12/84 (H)
64-17978	9/3/68	19/9/68
	16/6/71	20/7/72 (written-off landing at Kadena)
64-17979	21/4/68	25/9/69
	13/6/71	12/8/72
	13/7/76	13/8/77
	2/8/79 (H)	5/9/80 (H)
	3/7/88 (H)	12/8/88 (H)
64-17980	12/9/68	19/4/69
	19/6/71	15/8/72
	6/6/82	13/11/82 (H)

Note – (H) denotes that the SR-71 flew an operational mission on its positioning flight to Kadena from Beale, or as it redeployed from Kadena back to Beale. The first SR-71 to do this was '976', flown by Majs Al Cirino and Bruce Liebman, which flew an operational mission during its return flight to Beale on 9 August 1977. The next day, Majs Maury Rosenberg and Al Payne arrived at Kadena in '960', having successfully completed the first operational sortie en route to Kadena from Beale.

INSTRUMENT PANEL (Pilot's Cockpit)

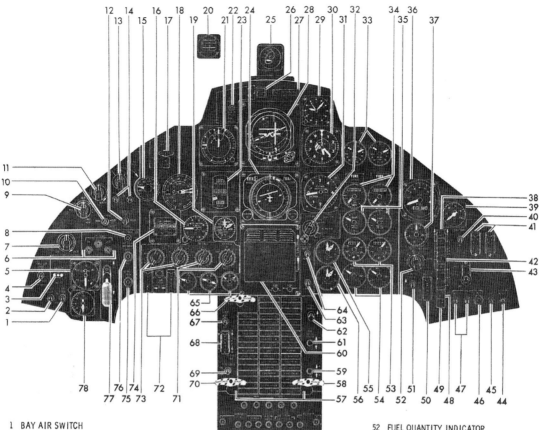

1 BAY AIR SWITCH
2 COCKPIT PRESSURE DUMP SWITCH
3 LANDING AND TAXI LIGHT SWITCH
4 MANIFOLD TEMPERATURE SWITCH
5 CABIN ALTIMETER
6 LANDING GEAR INDICATOR LIGHTS
7 SUIT HEAT RHEOSTAT
8 BRAKE SWITCH
9 FACE HEAT RHEOSTAT
10 COCKPIT TEMPERATURE SELECTOR
   AND OVERRIDE SWITCH
11 COCKPIT TEMPERATURE CONTROL
   RHEOSTAT
12 DEFOG SWITCH
13 TEMPERATURE INDICATOR SELECTOR
   SWITCH
14 L AND R REFRIGERATION SWITCHES
15 TEMPERATURE INDICATOR
16 ACCELEROMETER
17 DRAG CHUTE SWITCH
18 COMPRESSOR INLET PRESSURE GAGE
19 COMPRESSOR INLET TEMPERATURE
   GAGE
20 STANDBY COMPASS
21 AIRSPEED - MACH METER
22 AIR REFUEL SWITCH
23 TRIPLE DISPLAY INDICATOR
24 HORIZONTAL SITUATION INDICATOR
25 ANGLE OF ATTACK INDICATOR
26 AIR REFUEL READY - DISC
   PUSHBUTTON AND LIGHT

27 MASTER CAUTION LIGHT
28 ATTITUDE - DIRECTOR INDICATOR
29 ELAPSED TIME CLOCK
30 ALTIMETER
31 RATE OF CLIMB INDICATOR
32 DISPLAY MODE SELECTOR SWITCH
33 TACHOMETERS
34 EXHAUST GAS TEMPERATURE
   INDICATORS
35 EXHAUST NOZZLE POSITION
   INDICATORS
36 FUEL QUANTITY INDICATOR
37 FUEL TANK PRESSURE INDICATOR
38 FUEL CROSSFEED SWITCH
39 LIQUID NITROGEN QUANTITY
   INDICATOR
40 FUEL FORWARD TRANSFER SWITCH
41 EMERGENCY FUEL SHUTOFF SWITCHES
42 FUEL BOOST PUMP SWITCHES
43 FUEL DUMP SWITCH
44 INSTRUMENT INVERTER SWITCH
45 BATTERY SWITCH
46 GENERATOR BUS TIE SWITCH
47 L AND R GENERATOR SWITCHES
48 PUMP RELEASE SWITCH
49 FUEL BOOST PUMP LIGHTS TEST
   SWITCH
50 RSO BAILOUT SWITCH
51 IGNITER PURGE SWITCH

52 FUEL QUANTITY INDICATOR
   SELECTOR SWITCH
53 FUEL FLOW INDICATORS
54 OIL PRESSURE INDICATORS
55 L AND R HYDRAULIC SYSTEMS
   PRESSURE GAGE
56 A AND B HYDRAULIC SYSTEMS
   PRESSURE GAGE
57 ANNUNCIATOR PANEL
58 LANDING GEAR RELEASE HANDLE
59 YAW LOGIC OVERRIDE SWITCH
60 MAP PROJECTOR
61 PITCH LOGIC OVERRIDE SWITCH
62 BACKUP PITCH DAMPER SWITCH
63 ATTITUDE REFERENCE SELECTOR
   SWITCH
64 BEARING SELECT SWITCH
65 PITCH, ROLL, YAW TRIM INDICATORS
66 SURFACE LIMITER HANDLE
67 PITOT HEAT SWITCH
68 HYDRAULIC RESERVE OIL SWITCH
69 TRIM POWER SWITCH
70 EMERGENCY CHUTE DEPLOY HANDLE
71 INLET FORWARD BYPASS SWITCHES
72 EMERGENCY SPIKE SWITCHES
73 SPIKE SWITCHES
74 UHF CHANNEL FREQUENCY INDICATOR
75 INDICATORS AND LIGHT TEST SWITCH
76 GEAR SIGNAL RELEASE SWITCH
77 LANDING GEAR LEVER
78 LIQUID OXYGEN QUANTITY INDICATOR

Plate 1 – Front Cockpit

INSTRUMENT PANEL - Aft Cockpit

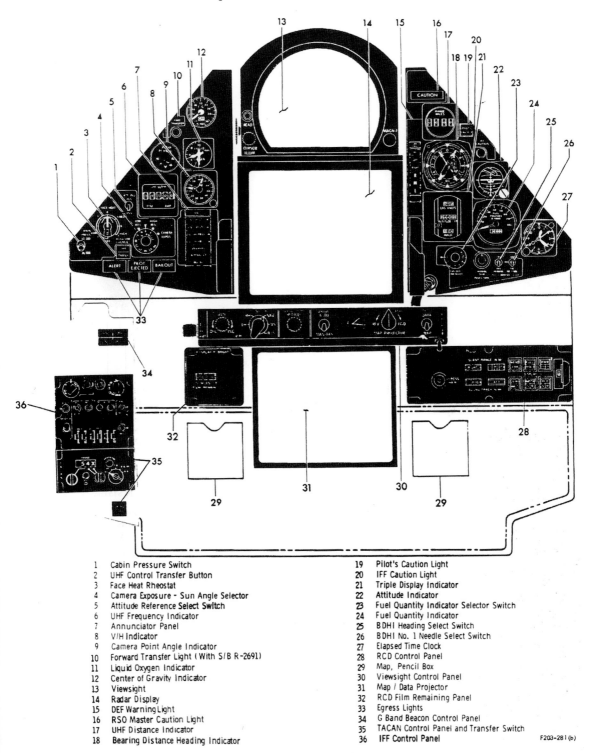

1	Cabin Pressure Switch	19	Pilot's Caution Light
2	UHF Control Transfer Button	20	IFF Caution Light
3	Face Heat Rheostat	21	Triple Display Indicator
4	Camera Exposure - Sun Angle Selector	22	Attitude Indicator
5	Attitude Reference Select Switch	23	Fuel Quantity Indicator Selector Switch
6	UHF Frequency Indicator	24	Fuel Quantity Indicator
7	Annunciator Panel	25	BDHI Heading Select Switch
8	V/H Indicator	26	BDHI No. 1 Needle Select Switch
9	Camera Point Angle Indicator	27	Elapsed Time Clock
10	Forward Transfer Light (With S/B R-2691)	28	RCD Control Panel
11	Liquid Oxygen Indicator	29	Map, Pencil Box
12	Center of Gravity Indicator	30	Viewsight Control Panel
13	Viewsight	31	Map / Data Projector
14	Radar Display	32	RCD Film Remaining Panel
15	DEF Warning Light	33	Egress Lights
16	RSO Master Caution Light	34	G Band Beacon Control Panel
17	UHF Distance Indicator	35	TACAN Control Panel and Transfer Switch
18	Bearing Distance Heading Indicator	36	IFF Control Panel

F203-281 (b)

Plate 2 – Rear Cockpit

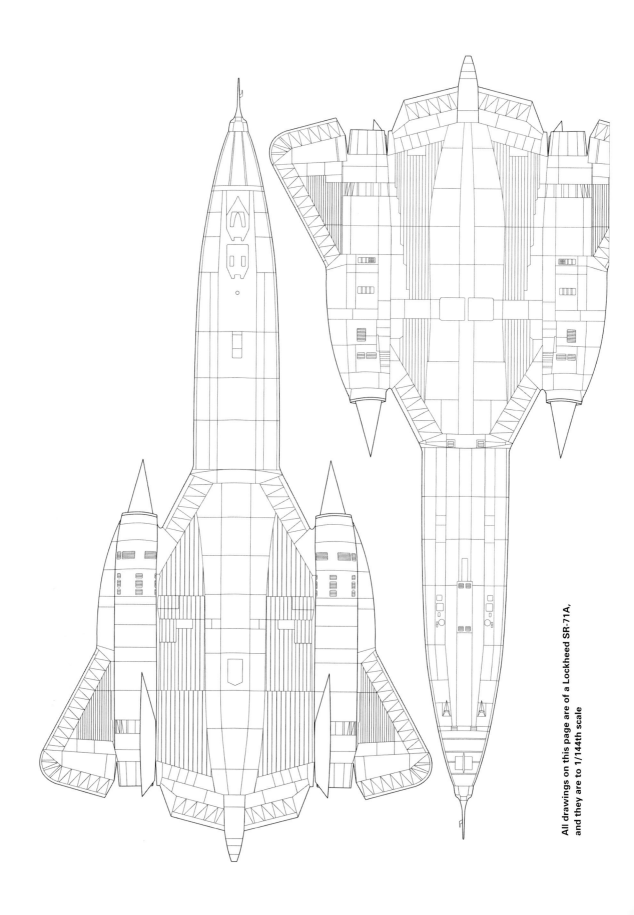

All drawings on this page are of a Lockheed SR-71A, and they are to 1/144th scale

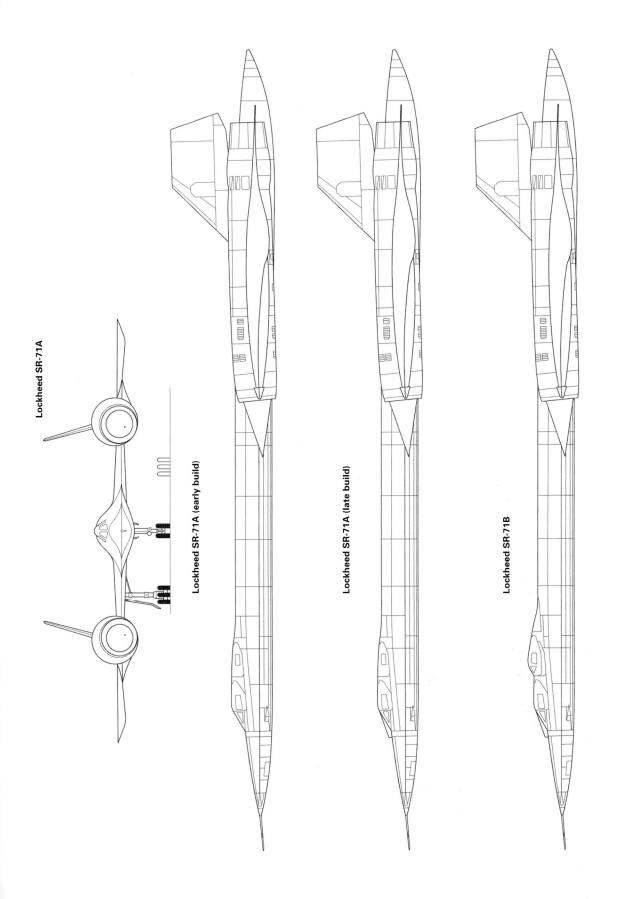

Lockheed SR-71A

Lockheed SR-71A (early build)

Lockheed SR-71A (late build)

Lockheed SR-71B

COLOUR PLATES

1

A-12 '77855' of the 1129th Special Activities Squadron, Kadena air base, Okinawa, October 1967

Operated exclusively by the CIA's 1129th Special Activities Squadron, the single-seat A-12 was the direct predecessor of the USAF's two-seat SR-71A. Conditions of great secrecy surrounded the deployment to Kadena air base, Okinawa, of three A-12s under the code name *Black Shield*. They flew a combined total of just 29 operational sorties before being returned to Area 51 and retired in 1968. All three operational aircraft were painted black overall, and were devoid of any national markings or insignia. Completely bogus five-figure serial numbers were applied to their twin-tail units, and to further confuse unwanted onlookers, these were changed from time to time in an attempt to hide the actual number of A-12s at the base. One Agency pilot recalls that the serials were painted in dark red, with first two digits always being 77 – '858', '835' and '855' were all used for a time.

2

A-12 Article Number 127 (60-6930) of the 1129th Special Activities Squadron, Groom Dry Lake, late 1963

A-12 Article Number 127 completed a total of 258 flights and 499.2 flying hours. It is seen here during the early flight test period in bare titanium finish. Black paint has been applied to the entire planform of the aircraft in an attempt to hide the wedges of Radar Absorbent Material used to help reduce the aircraft's Radar Cross Section. 127 is now on permanent display at the Space and Rocket Center Museum in Huntsville, Alabama.

3

AT-12 Article Number 124 (60-6927) of the 1129th Special Activities Squadron, Groom Dry Lake, 1965

Article Number 124 completed 614 flights and 1076.4 flying hours. It was the only A-12 configured as a two-seat pilot trainer, and unlike the jet's single-seat stablemates, it was powered by two J57 engines, which capped its upper speed envelope to Mach 2. The jet also remained in bare titanium, with a black skirt. It can be seen today in the California Museum of Science in Los Angeles.

4

M-21 Article Number 135 (60-6941) of the 1129th Special Activities Squadron, Groom Dry Lake, 1966

Tagboard was the CIA's codename for a programme to convert two A-12's into two-seater M-21 triple-sonic launch platforms that, it was hoped, would enable the D-21 reconnaissance drone to secure high-value PHOTINT of remote targets in China. Depicted here is M-21 60-6941, which was written-off in a catastrophic mid-air collision with its drone on 30 July 1966. Lockheed test pilot Bill Park miraculously survived the incident, although his backseat Launch Control Officer Ray Torrick drowned in the subsequent feet-wet parachute landing.

5

YF-12A Article Number 1001 (60-6934), Edwards North Base, 1964

Three prototype interceptors based on a two-seat version of the A-12 were constructed and tested under a classified project named *Kedlock*. Known as the YF-12A, each was equipped with a Hughes ASG-18 Fire Control System (FCS) and three Hughes AIM-9 missiles. The joint test team comprised Air Force Systems Command (AFSC), Aerospace Defence Command (ADC) and Lockheed personnel. Note the camera pods beneath each of the engine nacelles that were used to record missile separation.

6

YF-12C (SR-71) Article Number 2002 (60-6937), NASA, Edwards AFB, 1972

This jet is in fact SR-71A 64-17951 Article Number 2002, which first flew on 5 March 1965 and accumulated a total of 796.7 hours. Loaned to NASA from 16 July 1971, it performed high-speed/high altitude tests before being placed in storage. The jet is now on display at the Pima Museum in Tucson, Arizona.

7

SR-71A Article Number 2018 (64-17967) of the 9th SRW's Det 1, Kadena air base, Okinawa, late 1977

SR-71A 64-17967 Article Number 2018 first flew on 3 August 1967, and when retired on 14 February 1990, it had accumulated a total of 236.8 hours. The jet was deployed to Kadena on three occasion, the first being on 14 August 1977 – it is not known when the aircraft carried the tail art depicted here. The machine is displayed at the museum at Barksdale AFB, Louisiana.

8

SR-71A Article Number 2025 (64-17974) of the 9th SRW's OL-8, Kadena air base, Okinawa, September 1968

SR-71A 64-17974 Article Number 2025 was the third of three 'Habus' that constituted the first operational deployment of the 9th SRW to Kadena. Crewed by Majs Bob Spencer and Keith Branham, '974' landed on the island of Okinawa on 13 March 1968 and subsequently notched up OL-8's fourth operational mission on 19 April. The aircraft was rotated back to Beale AFB on 16 September, having completed more operational sorties than its two sister aircraft during this six-month milestone deployment (11 operational sorties, plus three additional sorties that were terminated early due to serviceability issues). To celebrate '974's' achievement, its proud crew chief TSgt Don Person christened it *Ichi Ban* – Japanese for 'Number One'. During the deployment, '974' also chalked-up a more questionable honour, as it was the first SR-71 to have been the confirmed target of an SA-2 SAM launch.

9

SR-71A Article Number 2029 (64-17978) of the 9th SRW's OL-KA, Kadena air base, Okinawa, July 1972
SR-71A 64-17978 Article Number 2029 was the first of three 'Habus' to undertake the inaugural operational deployment of the jet by the 9th SRW to Kadena. Crewed by Majs Buddy Brown and Dave Jensen, the jet arrived at its temporary operating location OL-8 on 9 March 1968. It had been planned that this crew and aircraft would also fly the first operational sortie over North Vietnam, but their scheduled mission was cancelled by higher authorities, so that honour went to Majs Jerry O'Malley and Ed Payne in 64-17976. The Playboy bunny – forever after known as 'Rapid Rabbit' – was applied to '978' early in its operational career, and still adorned the jet's twin tails when the aircraft was written-off in a landing accident at Kadena on 20 July 1972. Its crew (Majs Denny Bush and Jimmy Fagg) escaped unhurt.

10

SR-71A Article Number 2026 (64-17975) of the 9th SRW's OL-8, Kadena air base, Okinawa, June 1969
SR-71A 64-17975 Article Number 2026 was part of the 9th SRW's third operational rotation to OL-8. The five-and-a-half hour flight from Beale AFB to Okinawa was undertaken by Majs Jim Watkins and Phil Loignon on 24 April 1969. Majs Jim Hudson and Norb Budzinski flew '975' on its debut operational flight (over North Vietnam) on 11 May. The famous 'Black Cat' emblem depicted here on the tail of 975 actually belonged to a small hybrid Chinese Nationalist Air Force unit assigned to the 38th Reconnaissance Squadron that flew CIA-sponsored, highly classified (and dangerous), deep penetration U-2 missions over the Peoples' Republic of China from Taiwan. To date, it has proved difficult to determine the origins of this unique piece of tail art. One possible suggestion is that it could have been applied following a diversion into Taiwan.

11

SR-71A Article Number 2013 (64-17962) of the 9th SRW's Det 1, Kadena air base, Okinawa, January 1990
SR-71A serial 64-17962 Article Number 2013 was first deployed to Kadena by Maj Bill Campbell and Lt Col Al Pennington during Beale's second rotation to Southeast Asia, arriving in-theatre on 18 September 1968. The same crew christened '962' over the skies of North Vietnam on 30 September. It was the last SR-71 to leave Kadena following the shutdown of the *Senior Crown* programme, Majs Steve Grzebiniak and (RSO) Jim Greenwood departing the island 21 January 1990. The tail art says it all – the jet is the only 'Habu' to have been loaned to a museum outside the United States, '962' being displayed at the Imperial War Museum at Duxford, in Cambridgeshire.

12

SR-71B Article 2008 (64-17957) of the 9th SRW, Beale AFB, 1967
SR-71B 64-17957 Article Number 2008 was the second of two two-seat pilot trainers to be built, and it first flew on 18 December 1965. During a routine training sortie on 11 January 1968, the aircraft suffered a double generator failure. Despite being nursed back to Beale AFB using just back-up battery power for the aircraft's electrical system, it crashed on approach. Fortunately, both the instructor pilot, Lt Col Robert Sowers, and his student, Capt David Fruehauf, ejected safely.

ACKNOWLEDGEMENTS

The material for this book came from two basic sources – open literature and first-hand accounts from pilots, RSOs and people associated with the various programmes. Much of the information contained within these pages was gleaned from numerous interviews with those involved in Projects' *Oxcart*, *Kedlock* and *Tagboard*, as well as the *Senior Crown* programme. Several contributed information with the proviso that their anonymity be respected.

My grateful thanks therefore goes to Cols Don Walbrecht and Frank Murray, Denny Lombard, Dave Adrian, Bob Gilliland, Jim Eastham, Jay Miller, Jeff Richelson, T D Barnes, Cols Slip Slater, Buddy Brown, Don Emmons, Ed Payne, Tom Pugh, B C Thomas, Jerry Glasser, Frank Stampf, Buzz Carpenter, Curt Osterheld and Rod Dyckman, Lt Cols Blair Bozek and Tom Veltri, and Bob Murphy, Paul Eden, Jeannette Remak, Tim Brown, Steve Myatt, Robbie Shaw, Yefim Gordon, David Allison and Bob Dorr. I also wish to thank Maj Gen Pat Halloram, Brig Gens Dennis Sullivan and Buck Adams, Cols Tony Bevacqua, Pat Bledsoe, Larry Boggess, George Bull, Gary Coleman, Ken Collins, Dave Dempster, Bruce Douglass, Carl Estes, Tom Estes, Rich Graham, Ty Judkin, Joe Kinego, John Kraus, Jack Layton, Jay Murphy, Dewain Vick, Jim Watkins, Rich Young and Jack Maddison, Lt Cols Ben Bowles, Nevin Cunningham, Bill Flanagan, Jim Greenwood, Dan House, Tom Henichek, Bruce Leibman, 'G T' Morgan, Bob Powell, Maury Rosenberg, Tom Tilden, Ed Yielding, Reg Blackwell and 'Stormy' Boudreaux, Majs Brian Shul, Doug Soifer and Terry Pappas, and Keith Beswick, Kent Burns, Russ Daniell, Kevin Gothard, Graham Luxton, Lindsay Peacock, Dave Wilton, Betty Sprigg, Rich Stadler, Berni Mearns, Ellen Bendell, Steve Davies, Jim Goodall and Chris Pocock.

Finally, my eternal gratitude goes to my wife Ali, Dad, Neil and Pauline for their endless support and encouragement.

INDEX

Page numbers in **bold** denote illustrations.
Brackets show captions to colour plates.